W9-AXV-651

the worship choir resource

products available:

Choral Book	0-6330-8946-X
Listening Cassette	0-6330-8949-4
Listening CD	0-6330-8947-8
Accompaniment CD	0-6330-8948-6
(Split track: Voices right; Instruments left)	
Orchestration	0-6330-8950-8
CD Promo Pak	0-6330-9012-3
(Choral Book and Listening CD)	
Cassette Promo Pak	0-6330-9013-1
(Choral Book and Listening Cassette)	

Instrumentation: Flute 1-2, Oboe, Clarinet 1-2, French Horn 1-2, Trumpet 1-2-3, Trombone 1-2, Trombone 3/Tuba, Drum Set, Percussion, Harp, Rhythm, Violin 1-2, Viola, Cello, String Bass.

Substitute parts: Alto Sax 1-2 (substitute for French Horn), Tenor Sax/Baritone Treble Clef (substitute for Trombone 1-2), Clarinet 3 (substitute for Viola), Bass Clarinet (substitute for Cello), Bassoon (substitute for Cello), Keyboard String Reduction.

The rhythm part in this orchestration is designed to provide satisfying accompaniment throughout. However, keyboard players may find it helpful to reference certain passages in the choral score to supply the most supportive accompaniment.

GENEVOX

Scripture quotation on the back cover is taken from the *Holman Christian Standard Bible*, © Copyright 2000 by Holman Bible Publishers. Used by permission.

© Copyright 2002 GENEVOX, Nashville, TN 37234. Printed in the United States of America. Possession of a CCLI license does not grant you permission to make copies of this piece of music. For clarification about the rights CCLI does grant you, please call 1.800.234.2446.

my hat again goes off to our friends in the music world at LifeWay. I'm not saluting them for their sales records, product displays, or even their marketing savvy. I'm grateful to this ministry because I have a great sense that the core of what they want to do more than anything, for those of us in the world of music ministry, is to give us tools—tools for worship, tools for the body, tools that don't dumb down the awesome breadth of musical styles that God has given us, but tools that give us access to what is new and what is moving this generation into a wonderful new wave of worship.

I'm grateful to them because the tools I have most recently used from the hands of these capable men and women have been some of the most productive I have used

in a long time. *Jesus, the One and Only* not only met the broad-range needs of musicians in our music ministry, but it also struck a deep ministry chord in the hearts of those who listened.

I am confident that this new project, *The Worship Choir Resource,* is destined to give us all more of what we need for the week-to-week challenges that face us as worship leaders. They've included not only chorally challenging materials, but also songs that stand as congregational bridges to the corporate worship experience—that we all aspire to each week.

Martin Luther said it well when he said,

"Beside this, I am not of opinion that all sciences should be beaten down and made to cease by the Gospel, as some fanatics pretend; but I would fain see all the arts, and music in particular, used in the service of Him who hath given and created them."

May God give us all the skills to be good stewards of the art, and the greater skill, mixed with wisdom, to craft our art so that it feeds the souls of those who will listen.

Michael Adler
Minister of Music and Worship
Shades Mountain Baptist Church
Birmingham, Alabama

cOntents

Agnus Dei
(SATB)

Words and Music by
MICHAEL W. SMITH
Arranged by Dennis Allen

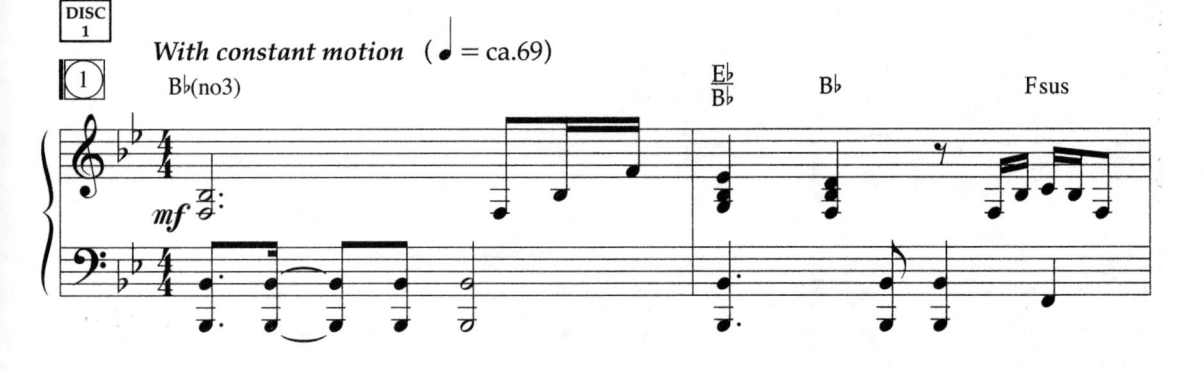

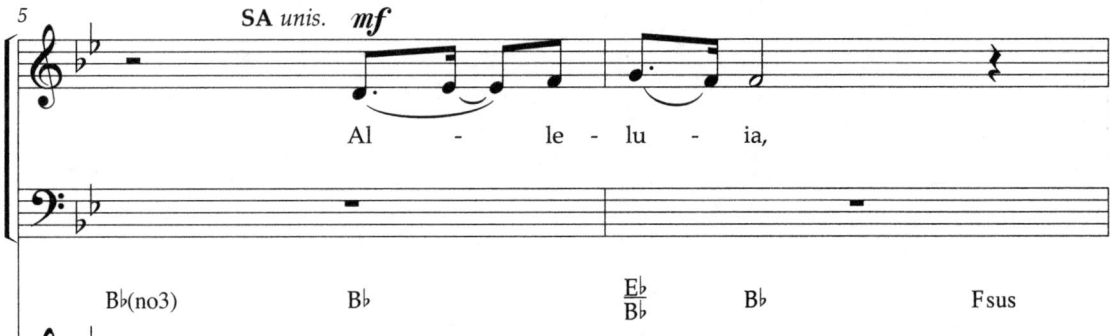

© Copyright 1990 and this arr. © 2001 Milene Music, Inc. (ASCAP).
All rights reserved. Used by permission.

8

For the Lord God Al - might - y reigns.

Al - le - lu - ia!

Ho - ly, ho -

12

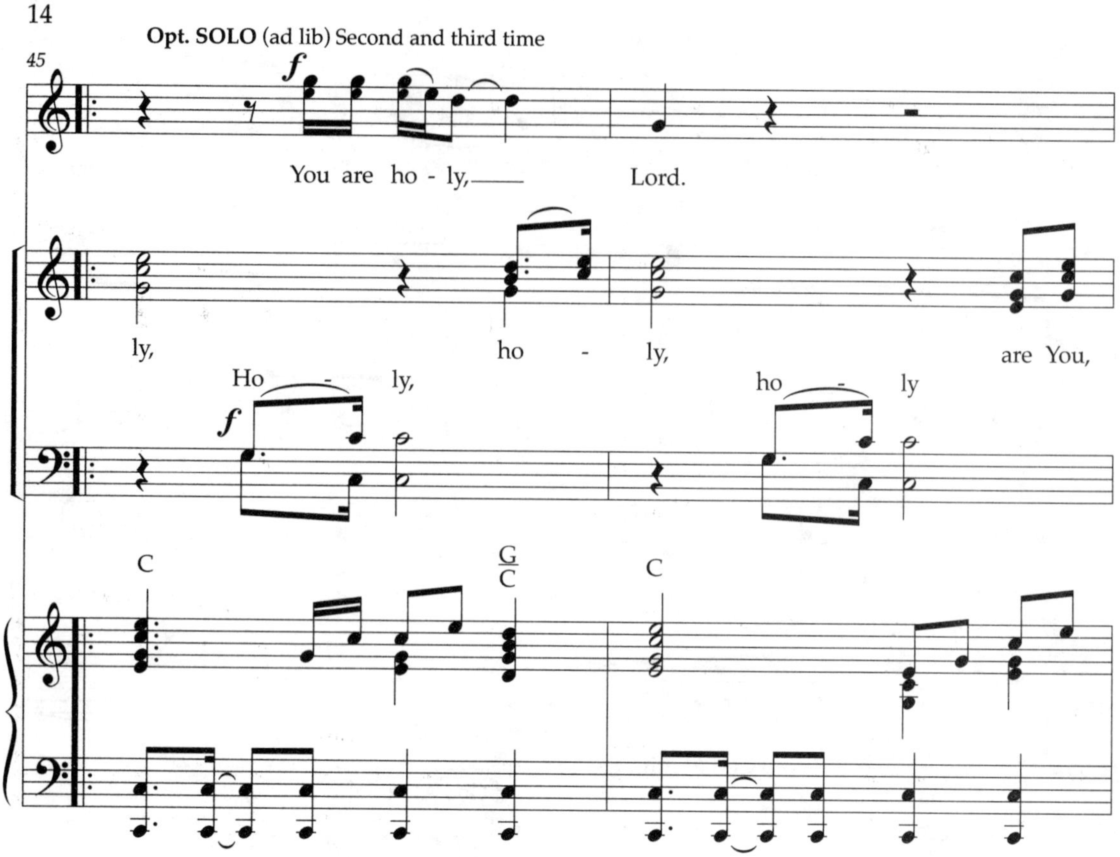
Opt. SOLO (ad lib) Second and third time
45
f
You are ho - ly,
Lord.
ly,
ho - ly,
are You,
Ho - ly,
ho - ly
f
C
G
C
C

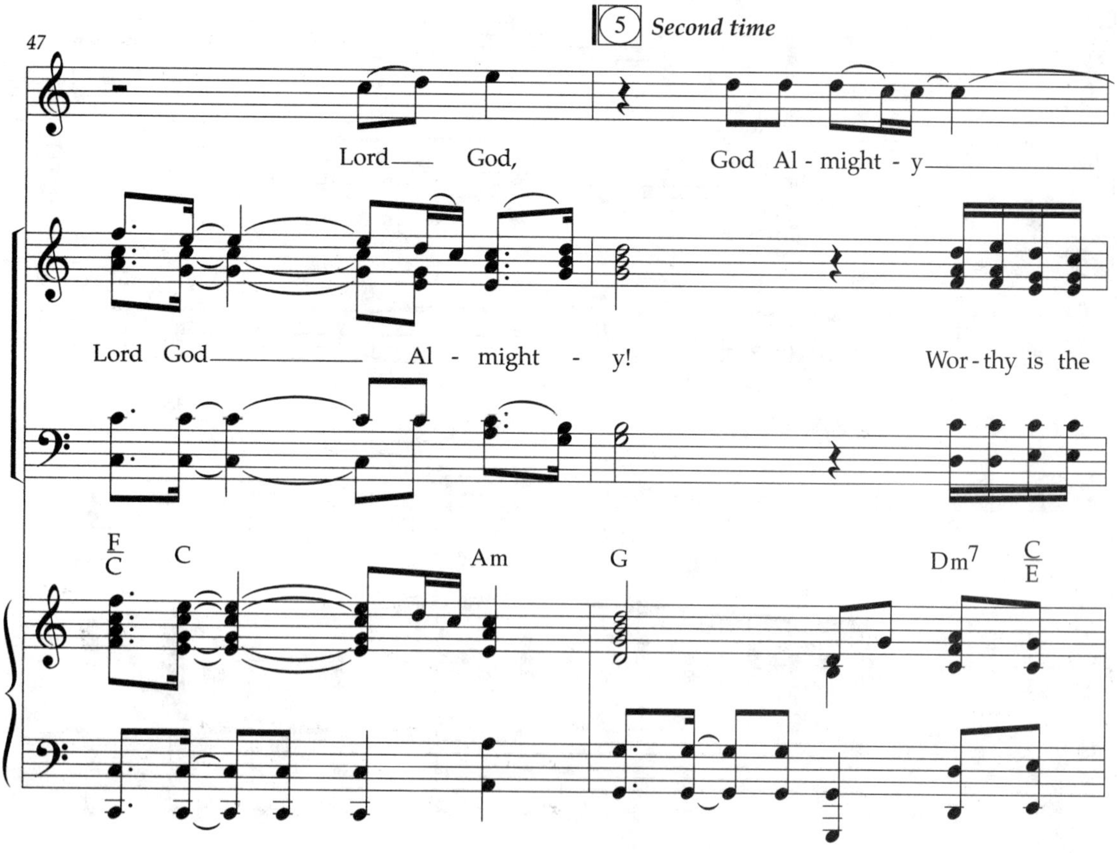
5
Second time
47
Lord God,
God Al - might - y
Lord God
Al - might - y!
Wor - thy is the
F
C
C
Am
G
Dm7
C
E

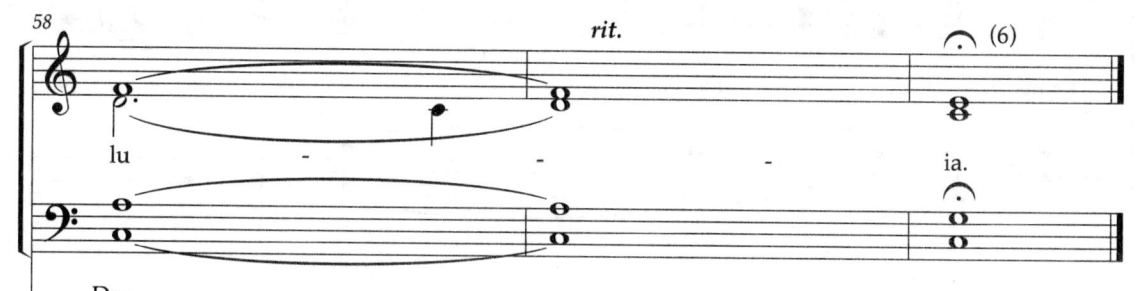

Forever
(SATB, Solo)

Words and Music by
CHRIS TOMLIN
Arranged by David Hamilton

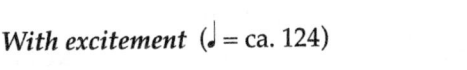
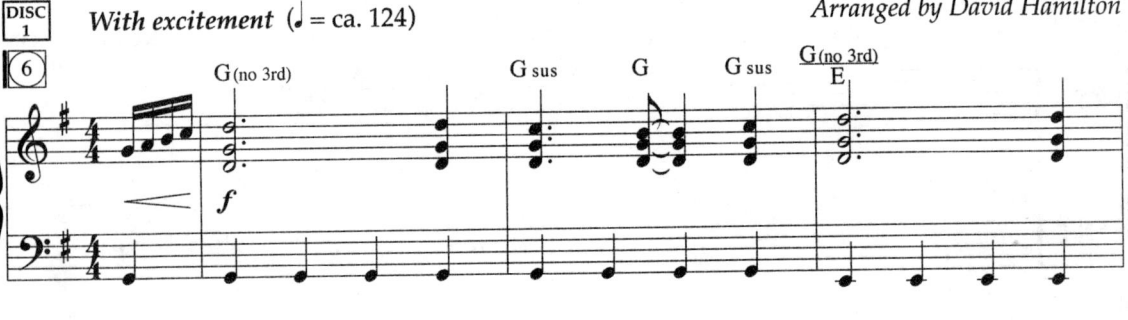

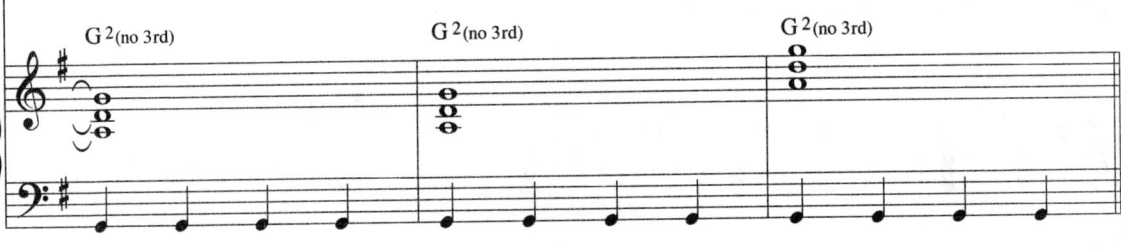

© Copyright 2001 and this arr. © 2002 worshiptogether.com/Six Steps Music (ASCAP).
All rights administered by EMI Christian Music Publishing. Used by permission.

13

thanks to   the   Lord,___   our   God   and___   King,___   His
might - y___   hand___   and   out - stretched_arm,___

CHOIR and CONGREGATION

mf

His

mf

G 2(no 3rd)   G 2(no 3rd)

15

love   en - dures__   for - ev   -   er.__   For He is good,_ He is a -
                                                                          For the life_____   that's

love   en - dures__   for - ev   -   er.__

G 2(no 3rd)   G 2(no 3rd)   C 2

Soloist may continue on melody

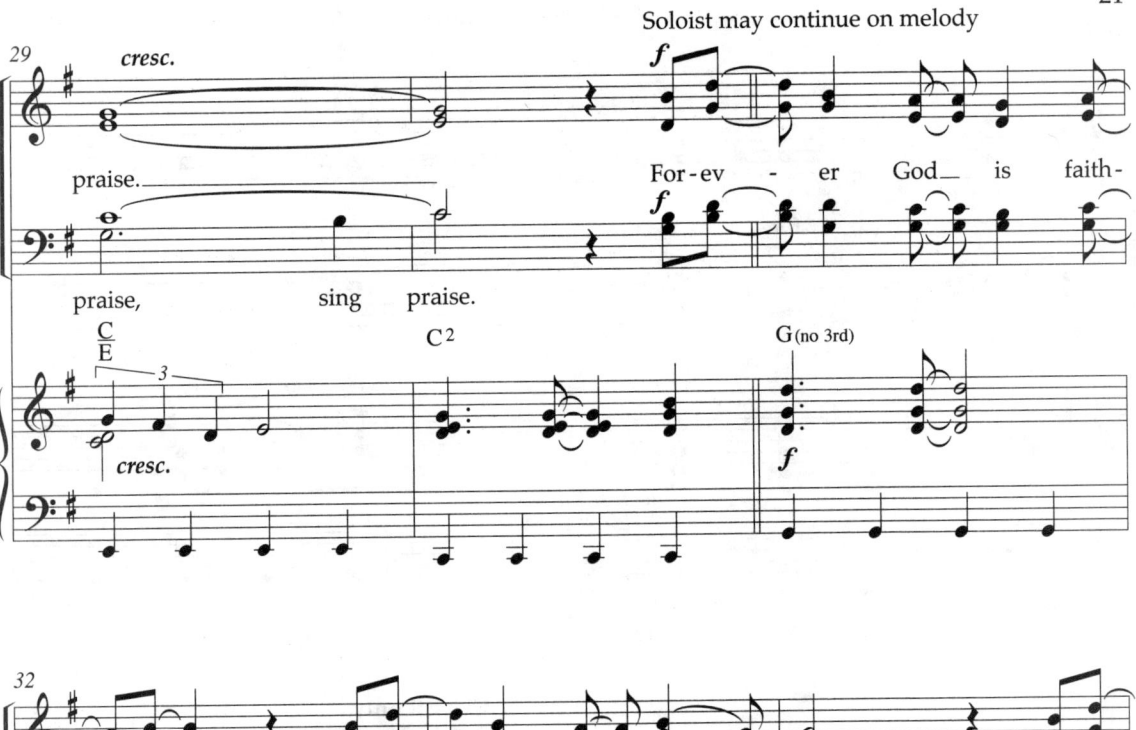

praise.

praise, sing praise.

For-ev - er God is faith-

- ful,___ for-ev - er God___ is___ strong, For-ev -

- er God___ is with___ us,___ for-ev - er___ and ev -

with CONGREGATION

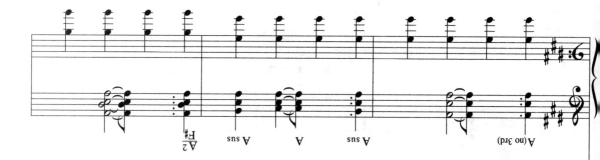
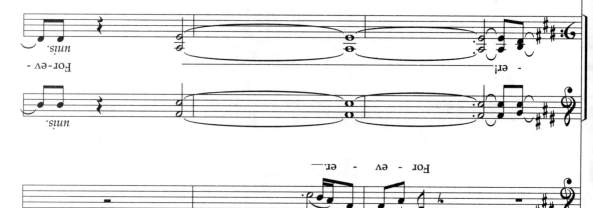

That's Why We Praise Him
(SATB)

Words and Music by
TOMMY WALKER
Arranged by Dennis Allen

© 1999 and this arr. © 2001 We Mobile Music (Administered by Doulos Publishing c/o THE COPYRIGHT COMPANY, Nashville, TN) / Doulos Publishing (Administered by THE COPYRIGHT COMPANY, Nashville, TN). All rights reserved. International copyright secured. Used by permission.

34

You Will Be Our God

(SATB)

Words and Music by
TRAVIS COTTRELL
and DAVID MOFFITT
Arranged by Travis Cottrell

© Copyright 2002 First Hand Revelation (ASCAP) and Van Ness Press, Inc. (ASCAP).
All rights admin. by LifeWay Christian Resources. All rights reserved.

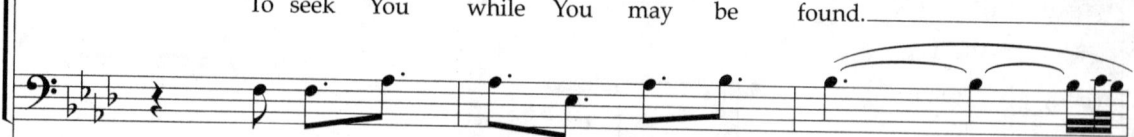

13
pas - sion with-in us to be where You are for -
A♭2(no 3rd)
A♭sus
A♭
15
ev - er - more.
So we cry out for mer-
TB unis.
C♭2(no 3rd)
D♭2(no 3rd)
D♭2(no 3rd)
Fm7
18
- cy,
we lay our lives down,
B♭2/D
Fm7
B♭2/D

To seek You while You may be found._____

And You will be our God_____ and

we'll be Your peo - ple for-ev - er_____ Be -

75
PRAISE TEAM
You will be, You will be our God.
er, for - ev -
Ab2(no 3rd)
Ebm7
Db2(no 3rd)
77
You will be, You will be our God.
er, for - ev - er, for -
Ab2(no 3rd)
Gb
Db2(no 3rd)/F
Ab2(no 3rd)

27

80

ev - er,_____ You will be our

E♭m7   D♭2(no 3rd)   D♭2(no 3rd)   A♭

83   unis.

You will be our God,_____

God,_____ we'll be Your peo - ple for - ev -

E♭sus   G♭

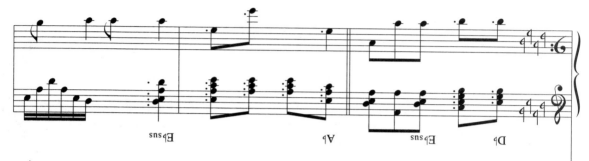

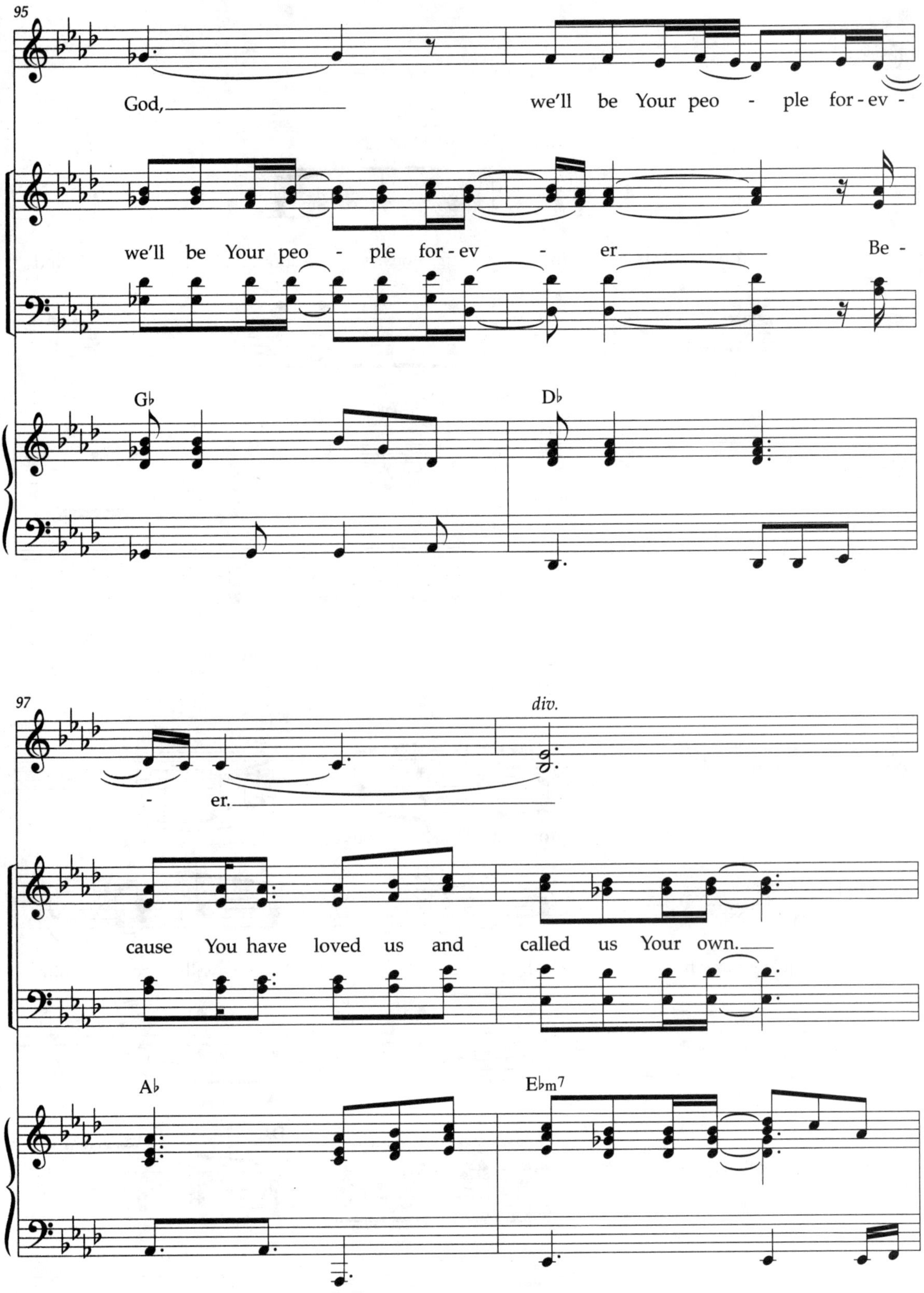

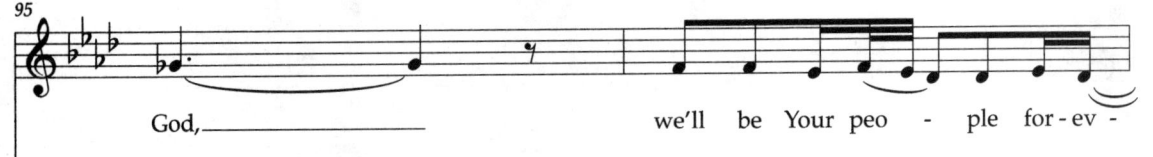

95
God,
we'll be Your peo - ple for - ev -
we'll be Your peo - ple for - ev - er
Be -
G♭
D♭
97
div.
- er.
cause You have loved us and called us Your own.
A♭
E♭m7

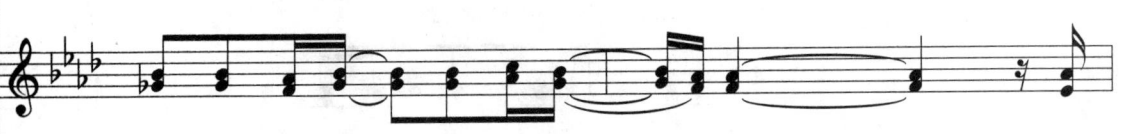

104
You will be our
God.
You will be our
God.
A♭
D♭
E♭
Fm/B♭
Fm2

107
God.
You will be our
God.
You will be our
D♭
E♭sus
A♭
D♭
E♭

110
unis.
div.
You will be, You will be our
God. You will be our
Fm
Eb/F
Fm
Db
Ebsus
Ebsus
Eb
8va
113
ff
God.
God.
Ab(no 3rd)
Ebm7
Db2(no 3rd)
Ab(no 3rd)
Ab
sfz

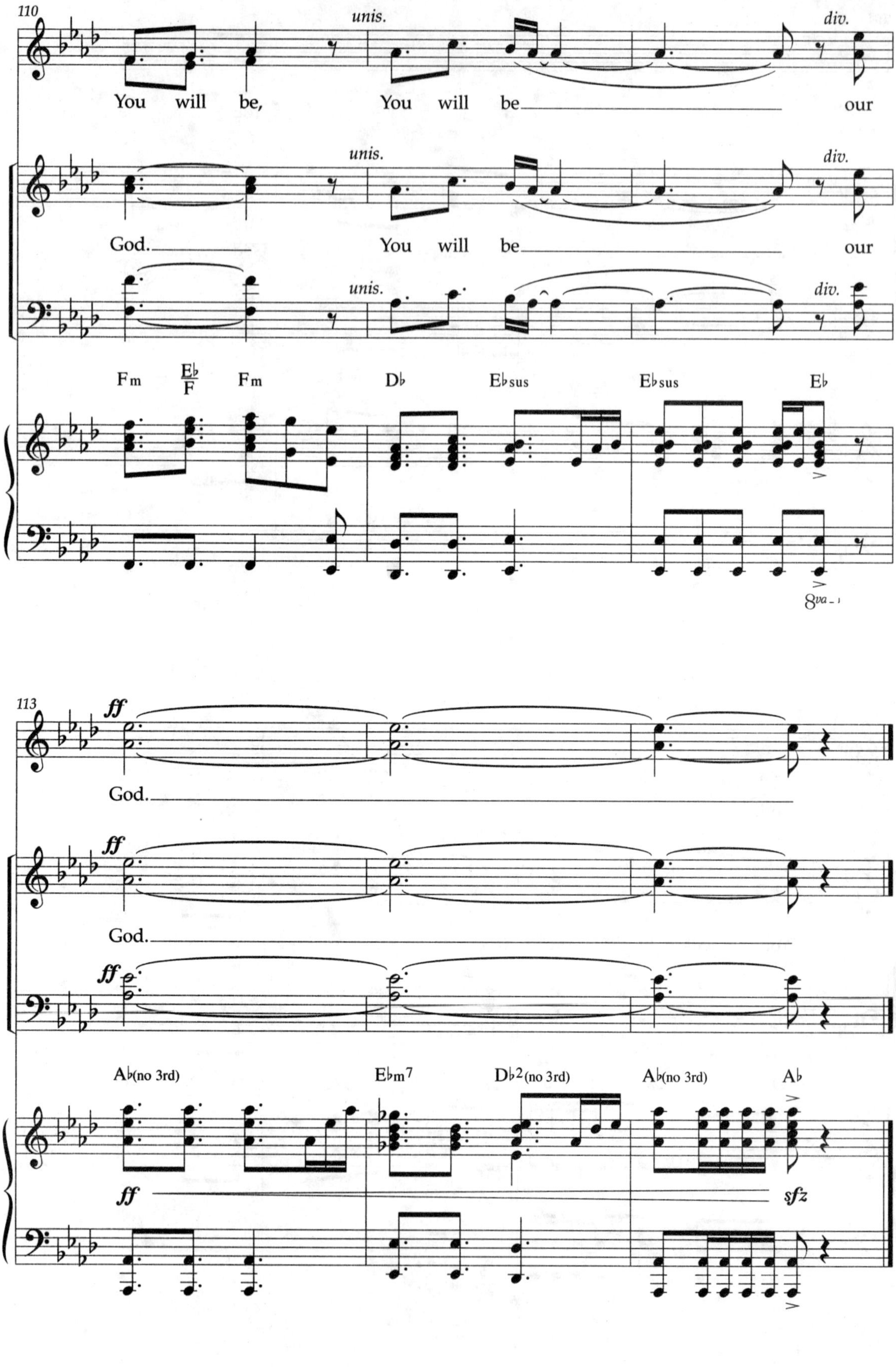

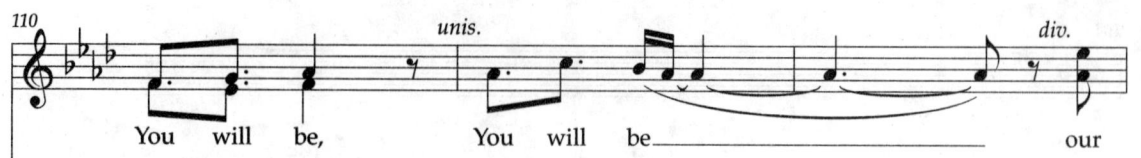

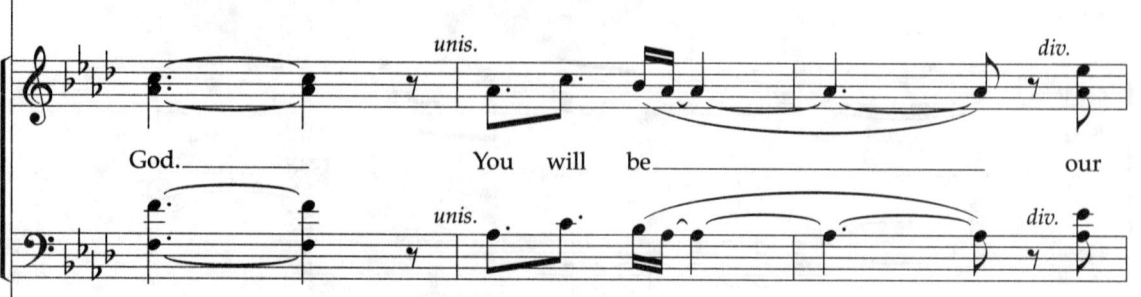

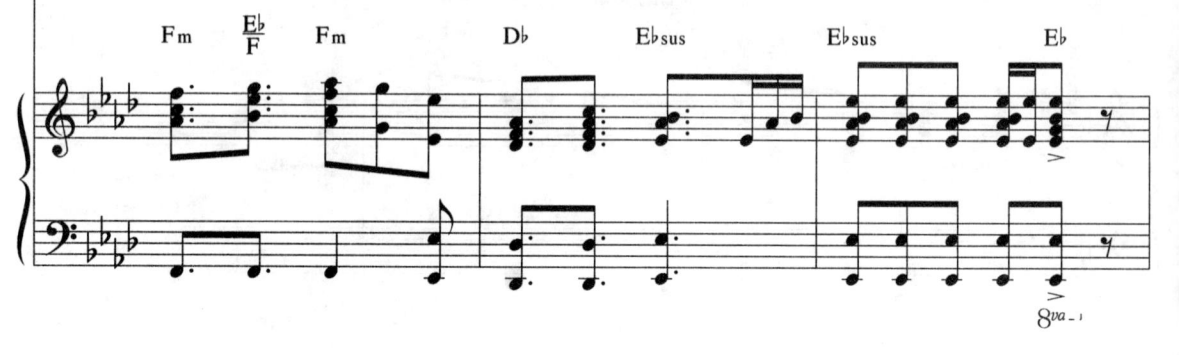

Knowing You
(All I Once Held Dear)
(SATB, Duet)

Words and Music by
GRAHAM KENDRICK
Arranged by Dennis Allen

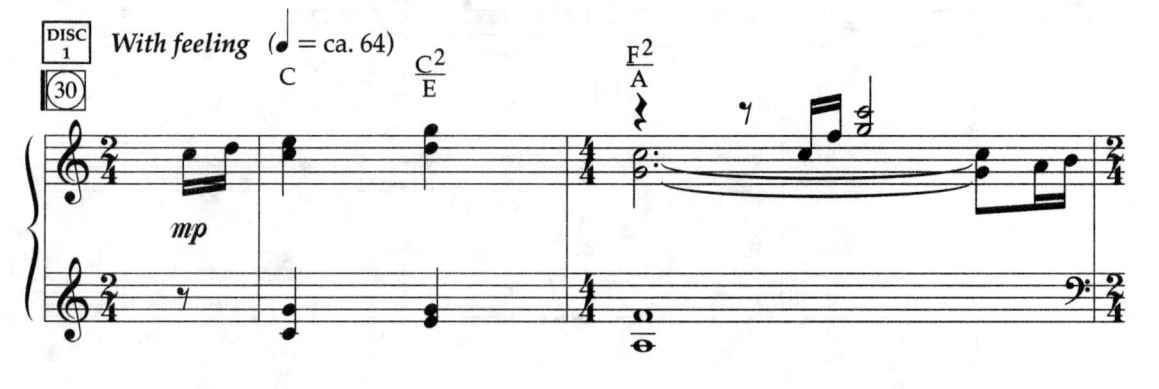

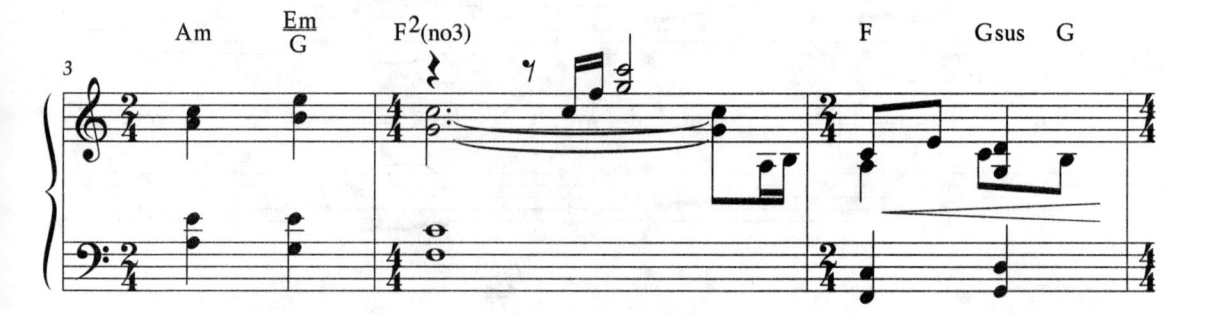

SOLO (opt. SA *unis.*) *mf*

1. All I— once held— dear, built my— life up - on, all this

© 1994 and this arr. © 2000 Make Way Music/ASCAP (Admin. in the Western Hemisphere by Music Services). All rights reserved. Used by permission.

58

No Greater Love
(SATB)

Words and Music by
TOMMY WALKER
Arranged by J. Daniel Smith

© Copyright 1993 and this arr. © 2001 Doulos Publishing (adm. by THE COPYRIGHT COMPANY, Nashville, TN)/Dayspring Music, Inc. (BMI). All rights reserved. Made in the USA. International copyright secured. Used by permission.

68

69

74

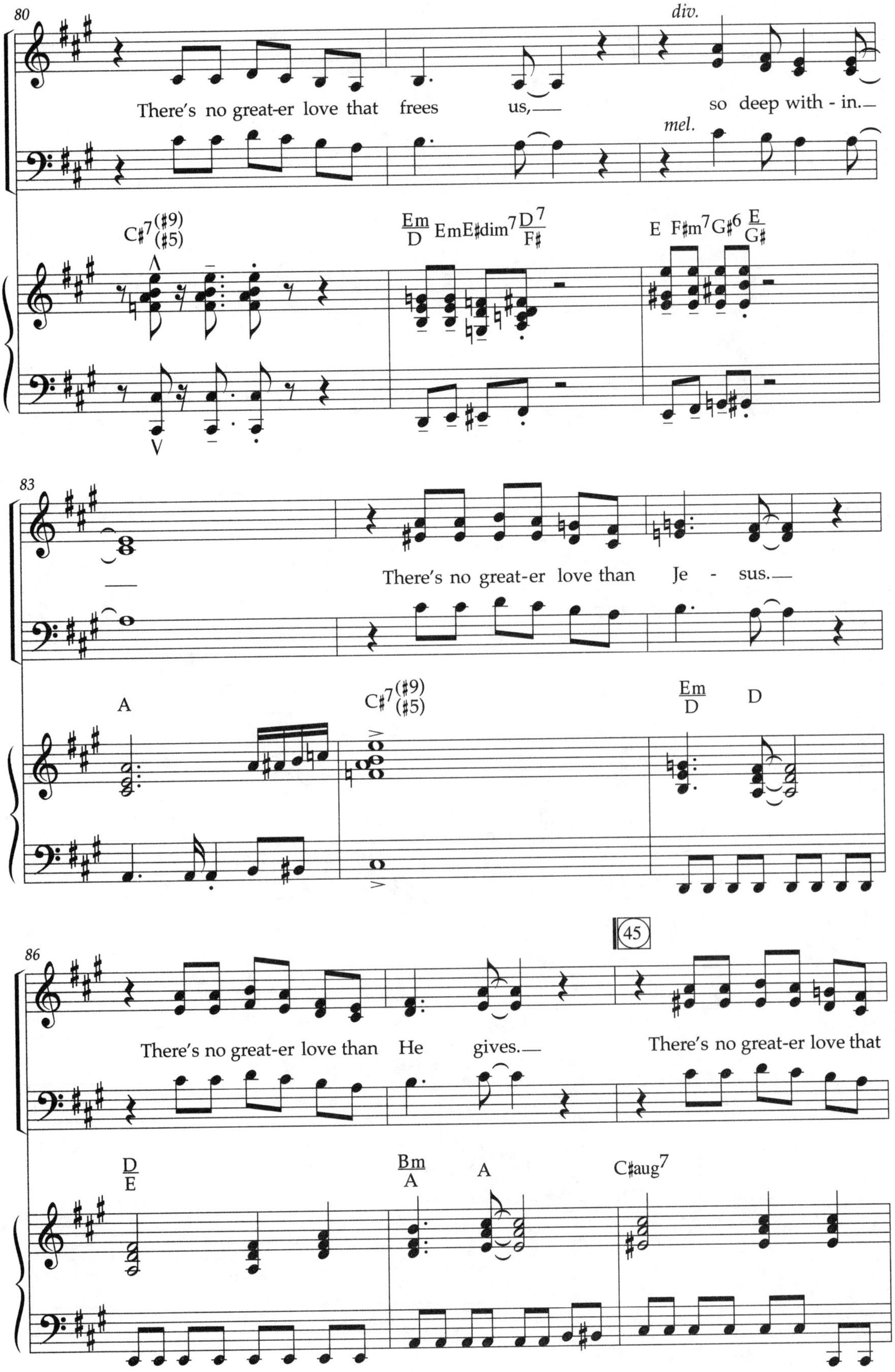

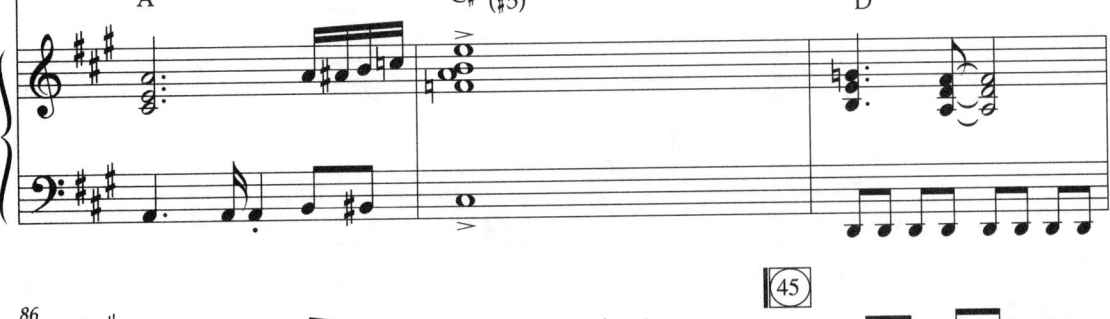

80
div.
There's no great-er love that frees us,—
so deep with - in.—
mel.
C♯7(♯9)(♯5)
Em/D EmE♯dim7 D7/F♯
E F♯m7 G♯6 E/G♯
83
There's no great-er love than Je - sus.—
A
C♯7(♯9)(♯5)
Em/D D
45
86
There's no great-er love than He gives.—
There's no great-er love that
D/E
Bm/A A
C♯aug7

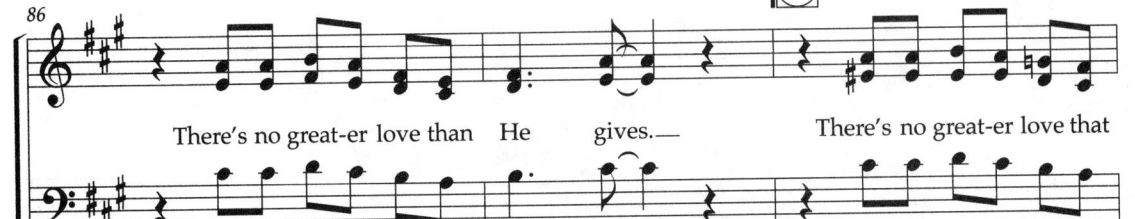

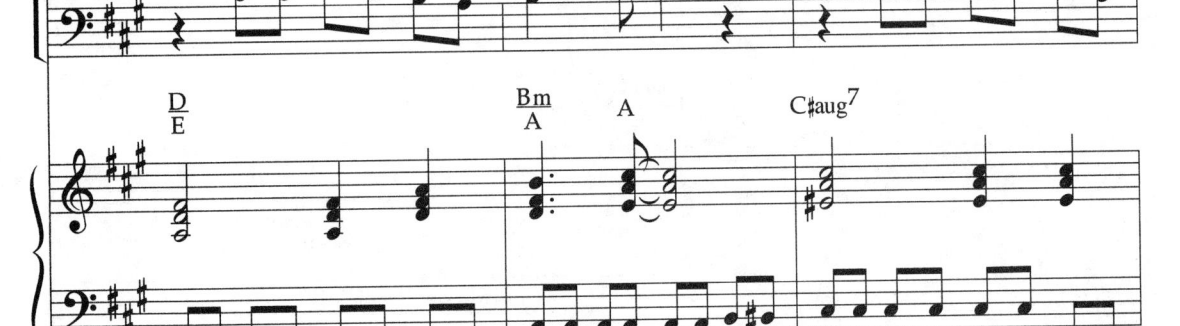

Power of Your Love
(SATB)

Words and Music by
GEOFF BULLOCK
Arranged by Steve Dunn

Lord, I come to You,___ let my heart be changed, re-newed,___

"And Can It Be," Music by Thomas Campbell.

© 1992 and this arr. © 2000 Word Music, Inc. (ASCAP)/Maranatha! Music (ASCAP)
(admin. by Word Music, Inc.) All rights reserved. Used by permission.

flow-ing from the grace that I've found___ in

You;

MEN *unis.* *mp* And, Lord, I've come to know___

the weak - ness - es I see in me;___

will be stripped a - way

[48]

by the pow'r of Your love.

Hold   me close,   let Your love sur - round

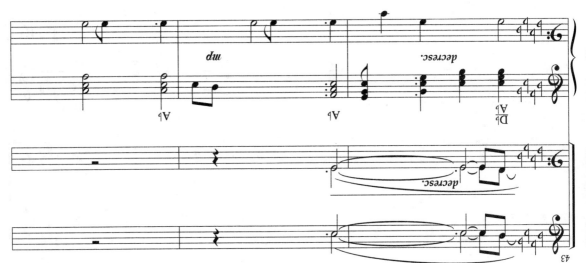

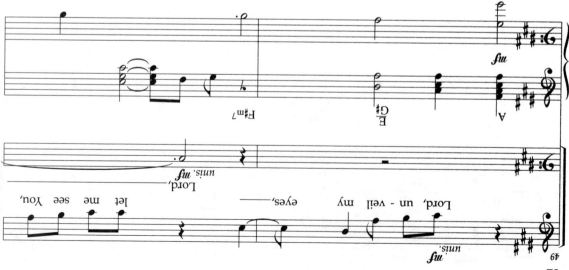

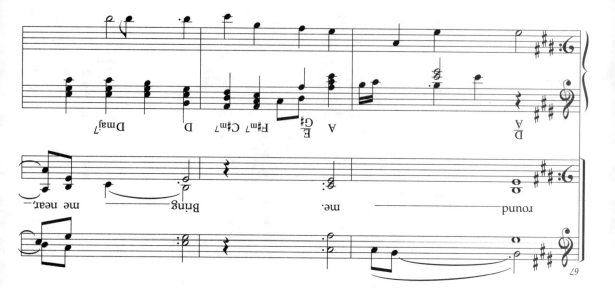
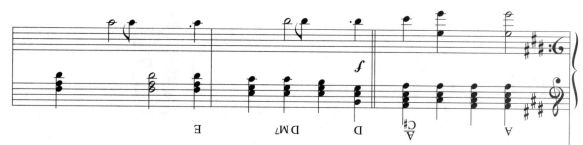

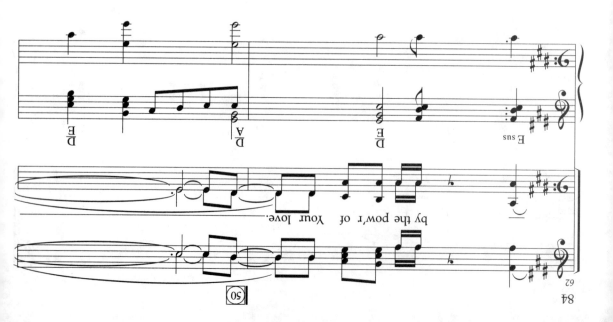

draw me to Your___ side;_____

side,_____ Your side;

And

as   I wait___   I'll rise up like the   ea   -

gle,   and I will soar with   You.   Your Spir - it   leads   me

I'll rise up like the ea - gle, and I will soar with You. Your Spir-it leads me on in the pow'r of Your love.

Praise to the Lord, the Almighty
(SATB)

Words: German Hymn, Joachim Neander
Trans: Catherine Winkworth

Music: *Stralsund Gesangbuch*
Arranged by Travis Cottrell
and Russell Mauldin

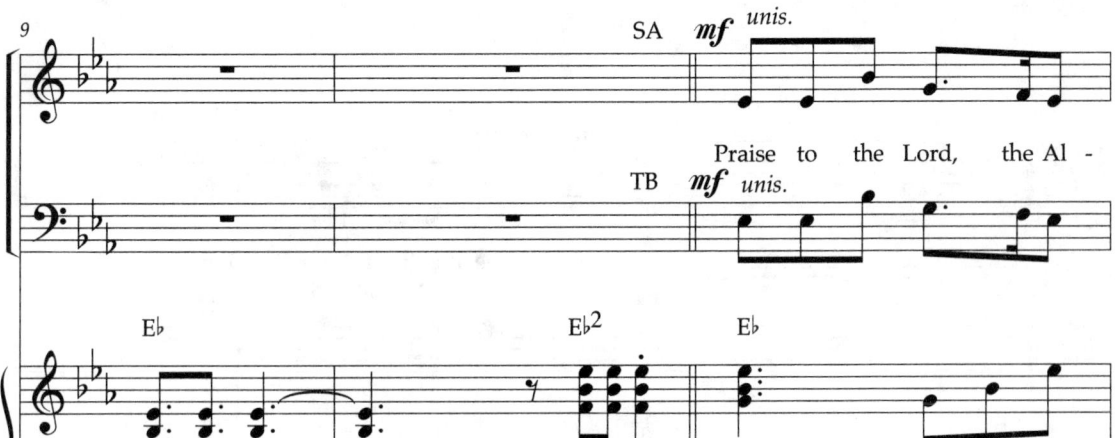

Praise to the Lord, the Al -

© 1999 and this arr. © 2000 First Hand Revelation (ASCAP)/Van Ness Press, Inc. (ASCAP).
All rights adminstered by LifeWay Christian Resources. All rights reserved.

*Original text: "Praise Him"

*Original text: "yea"
**Original text: "thy desires e'er"

Breathe
(SATB)

Words and Music by
MARIE BARNETT
Arranged by Don Hart

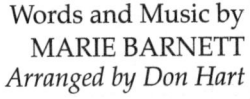

This is the air

© 1995 and this arr. © 2002 Mercy/Vineyard Publishing
(admin. by Music Services, Inc.)/ASCAP.
All rights reserved. Used by permission.

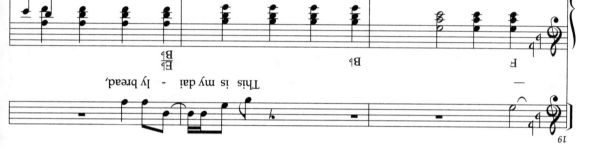

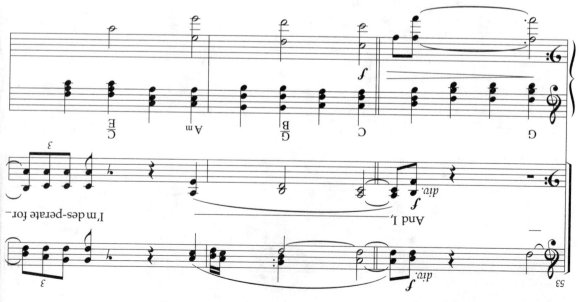

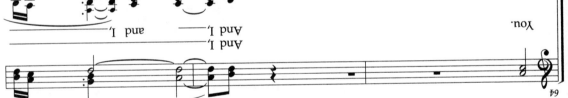

Firm Foundation

(SATB, Solo)

Words and Music by
NANCY GORDON and JAMIE HARVILL
Arranged by Gary Rhodes

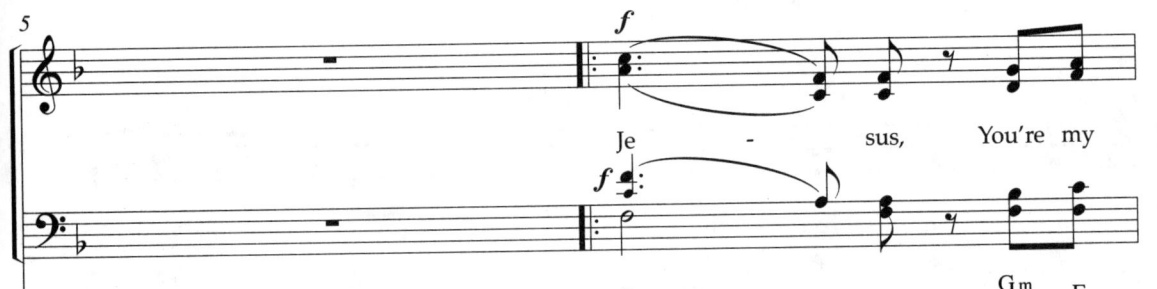

© Copyright 1994 Integrity's Hosanna! Music/ASCAP & Integrity's Praise! Music/BMI
c/o Integrity Music, Inc., 1000 Cody Rd., Mobile, AL 36695.
All rights reserved. International copyright secured. Used by permission.

15
1
2
ly Word.
ly Word.
C
F/C
F
N.C.
17
mf
Your Word is faith - ful,
mf unis.
F
C/F
19
Might - y in pow - er.
B♭
Gm7/D

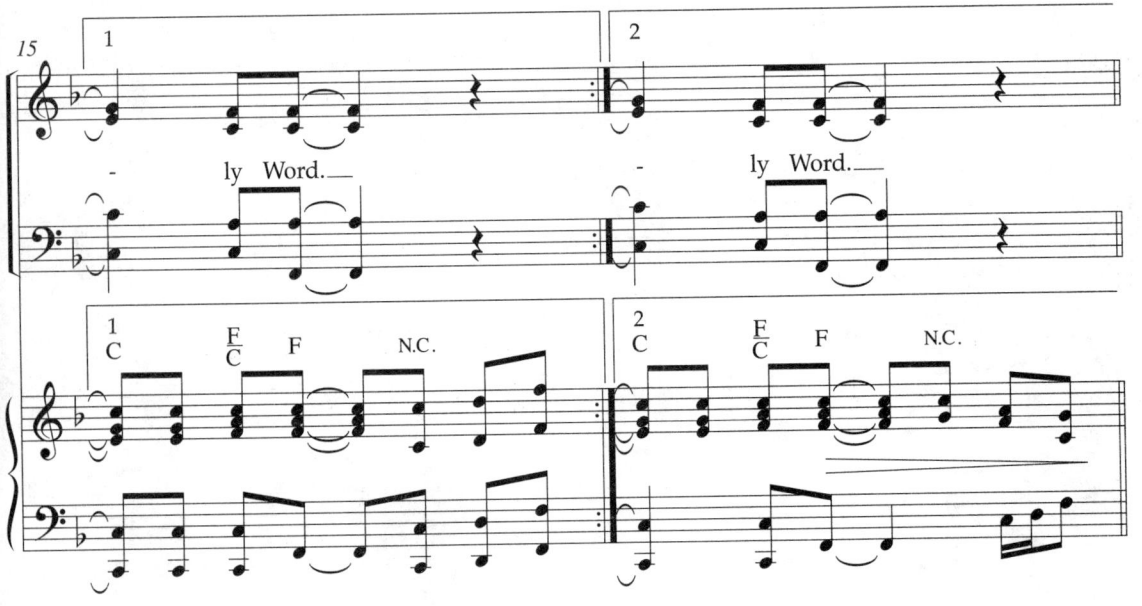

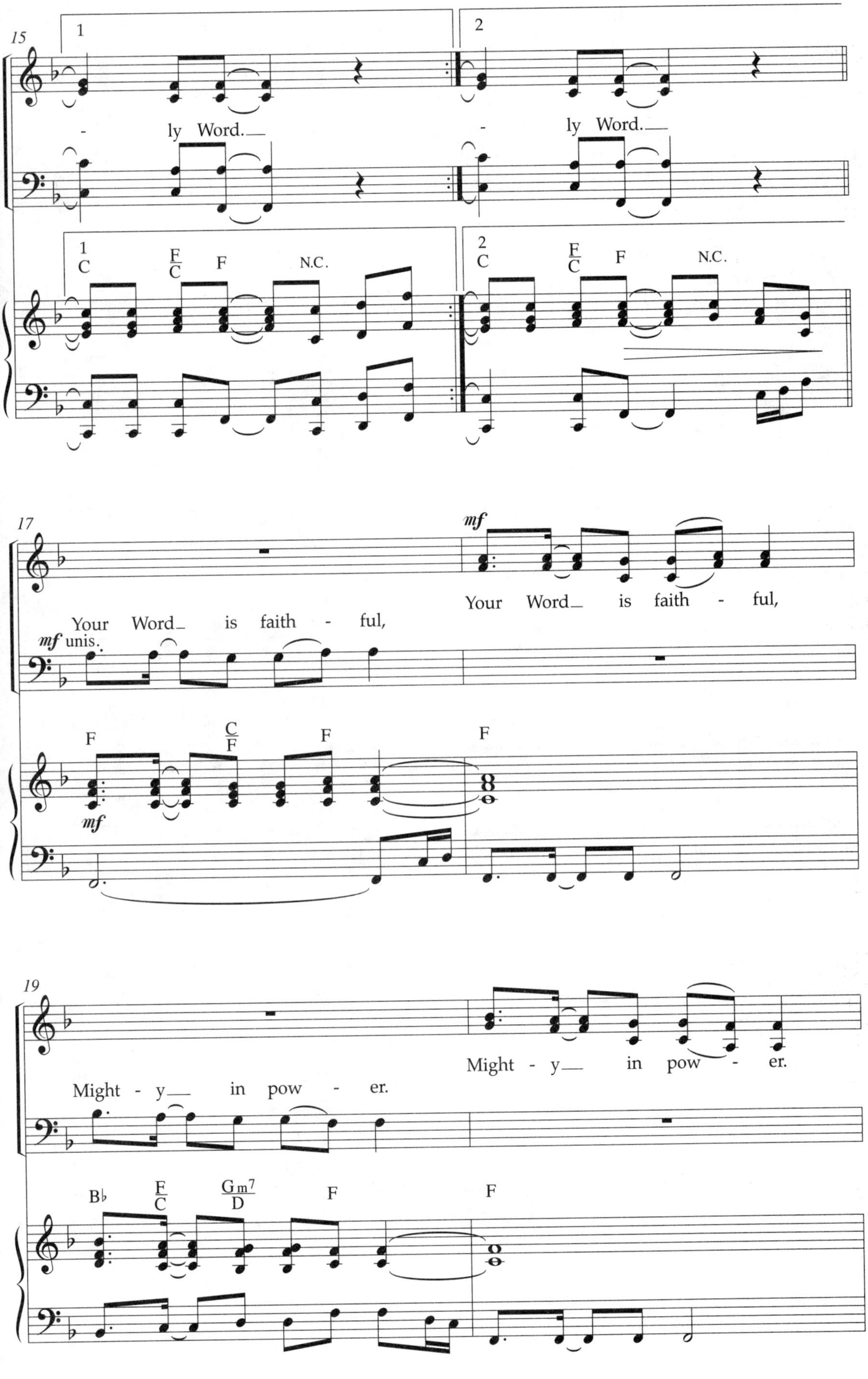

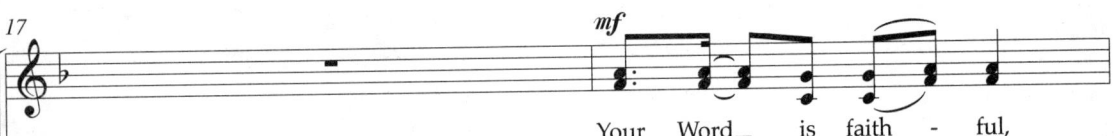

I know I can stand____ se - cure.____

Je - sus, You're my firm foun - da - tion;____

I put my hope in Your ho - ly Word.____

"The Church's One Foundation," Words by SAMUEL J. STONE, Music by SAMUEL S. WESLEY.

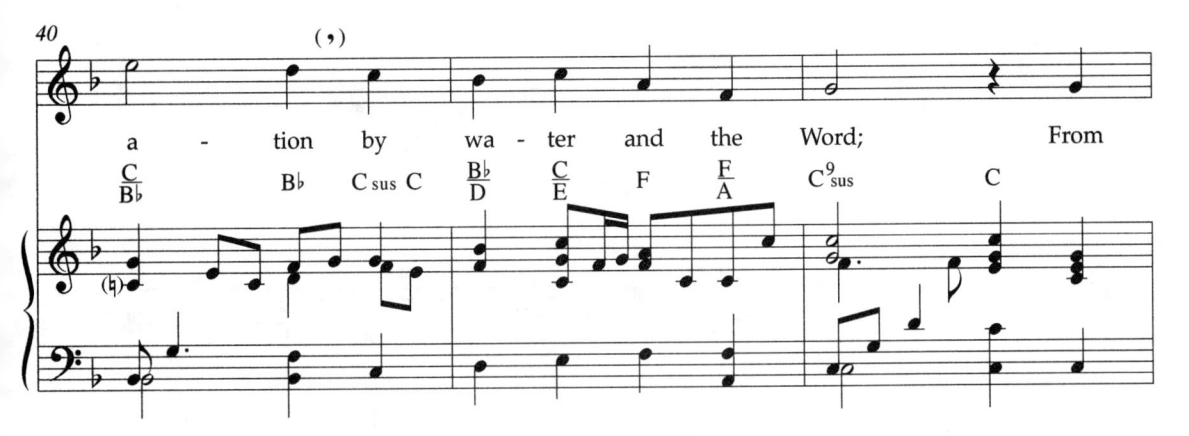

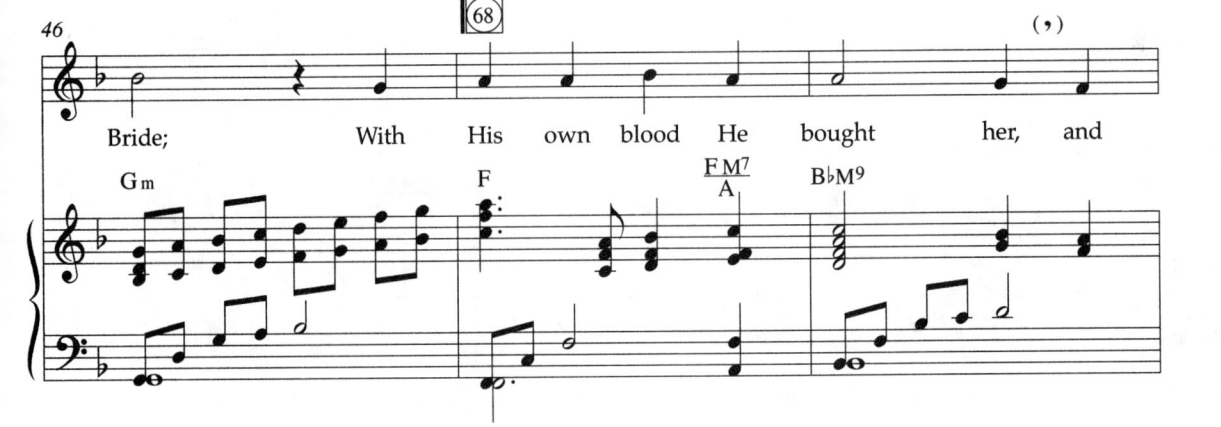

116

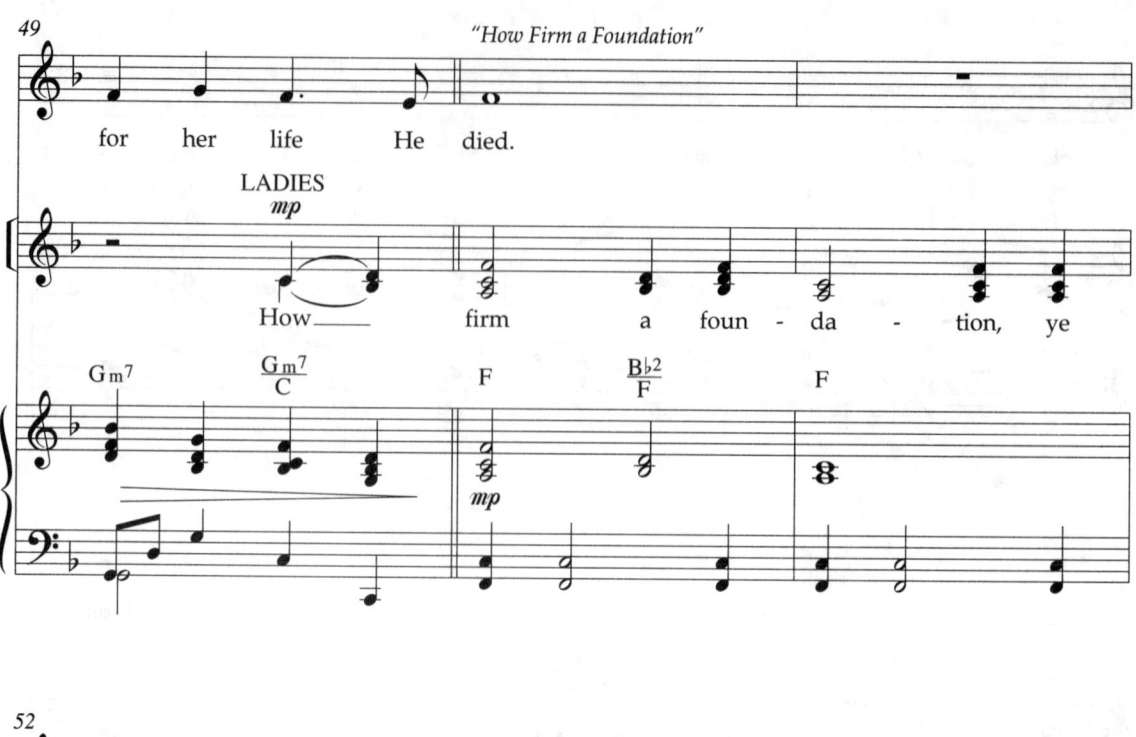

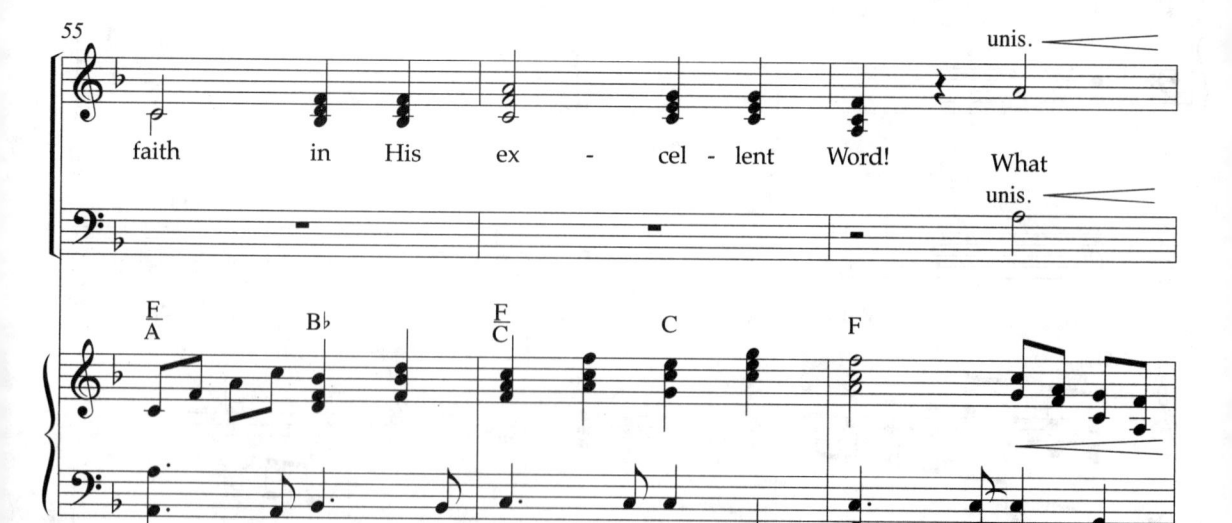

"How Firm a Foundation," Words from John Rippon's *Selection of Hymns,* Music from John Funk's *Genuine Church Music.*

Je - sus, You're my firm foun - da - tion;___

I put my hope in Your ho - ly Word.___

I put my hope in Your ho - ly Word.___

120

Jesus, I Am Resting, Resting

(SATB, Solo)

JEAN S. PIGOTT

DAVID HAMPTON
Arranged by Gary Rhodes

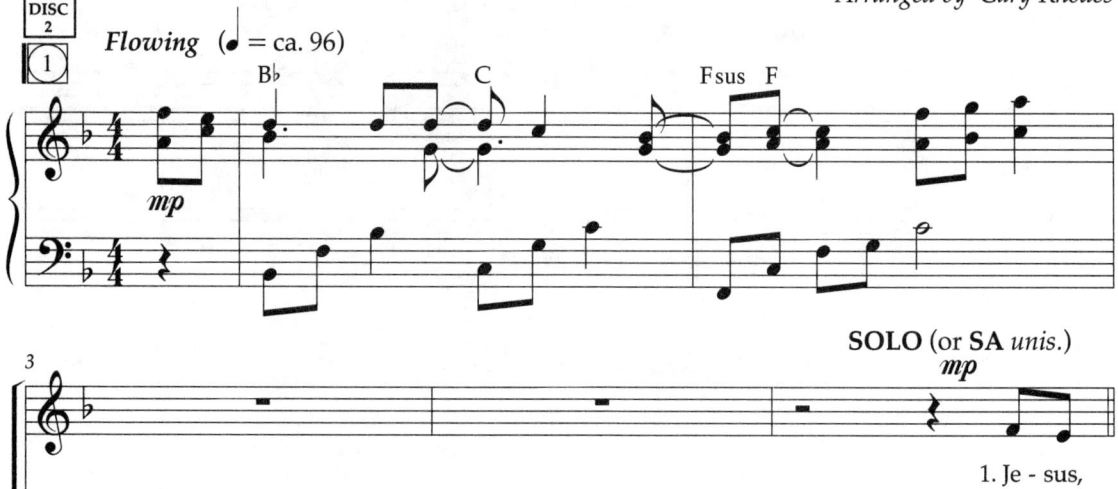

© Copyright 1998 and this arr. © Copyright 2000 New Spring Publishing, Inc. (ASCAP)
(a div. of Brentwood-Benson Music Publishing, Inc.) All rights reserved. Used by permission.

3 First time
5 Second time

ness Of Thy lov - ing heart.

Fsus F B♭maj9 Gm/C F

CHOIR unis. *mp* 2 rit. unis. *f*

2. Sim-ply 3. Ev-er
unis. *mp* unis. *f*

2 F E♭/F F Fsus F

mp *rit.* *f*

a tempo

lift Thy face_ up - on___ me As I work and wait_ for_ Thee;_

E♭2 F/A B♭sus B♭ E♭ F/A

a tempo

36
div.
Rest-ing 'neath Thy smile, Lord Je - sus, Earth's dark
div.
B♭sus B♭
E♭
F/A
B♭sus B♭
39
With bright countenance
shad - ows flee.
Bright-ness of my Fa - ther's glo -
B♭/E♭
Cm/F
B♭
E♭maj9
Fsus
B♭/F
42
- ry,
Sun-shine of my Fa - ther's face,
Keep me
B♭
Gm7
B♭maj7/F
E♭2
E♭

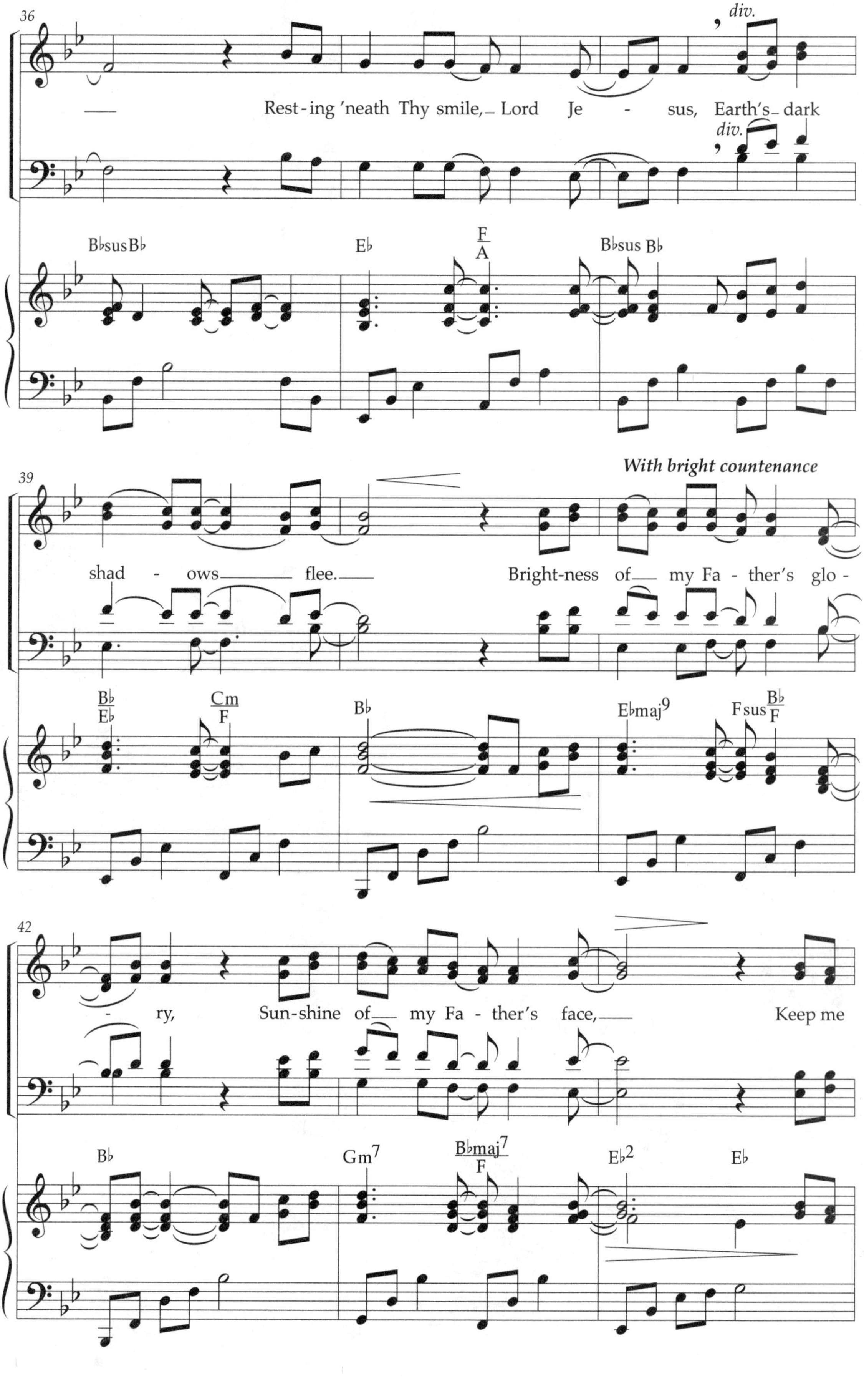

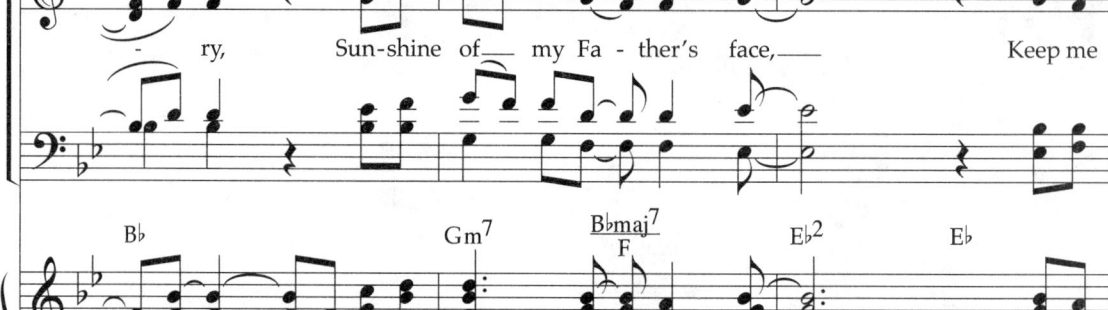

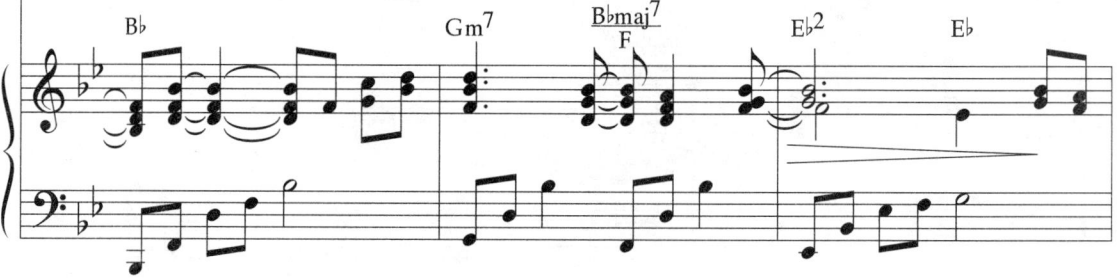

130

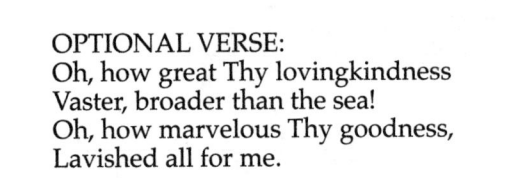

OPTIONAL VERSE:
Oh, how great Thy lovingkindness
Vaster, broader than the sea!
Oh, how marvelous Thy goodness,
Lavished all for me.

Yes, I rest in Thee, Beloved,
Know what wealth of grace is Thine,
Know Thy certainty of promise
And have made it mine.

Unto the King

(SATB)

Words and Music by
TOMMY WALKER
Arranged by Richard Kingsmore

© Copyright 2000 and this arr. © Copyright 2001 Integrity's Praise! Music/BMI, c/o Integrity Media, Inc., 1000 Cody Road, Mobile, AL 36695. All rights reserved. Used by permission.

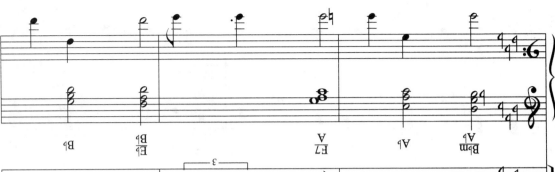

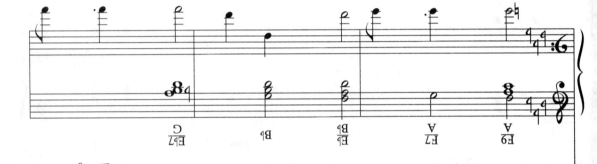

30
Hon-or and glo-ry and pow-er and might, be un-to Je-sus the
E♭ B♭ E♭7/G A♭ E♭/B♭
33
King. for-ev-er and ev - er,
unis.
Be all the hon - or, be all the glo-
B♭ A♭ E♭/B♭ B♭ A♭
36
for-ev-er and ev - er, for-ev-er and
- ry, all a-dor-a - tion,
E♭/B♭ B♭ A♭

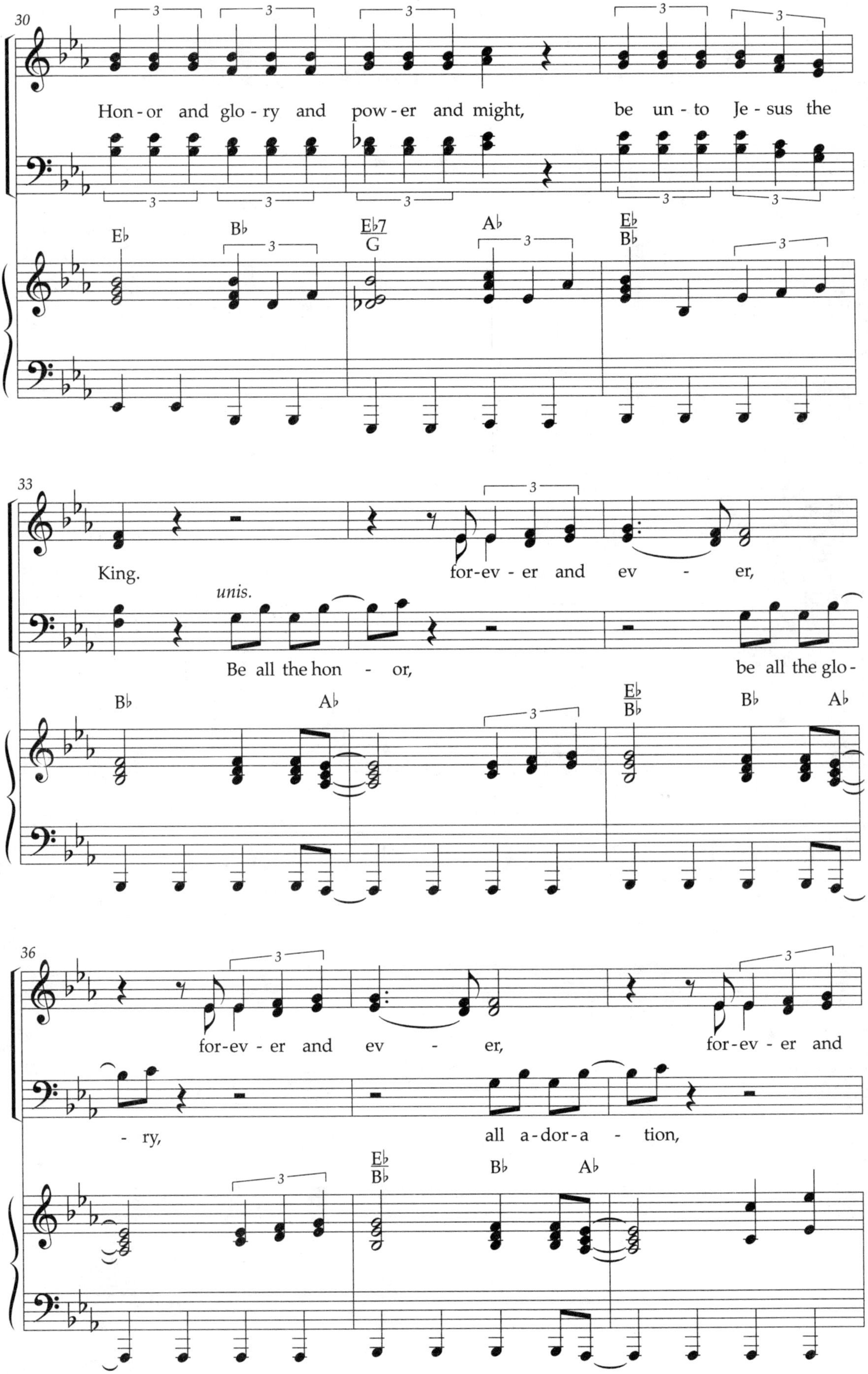

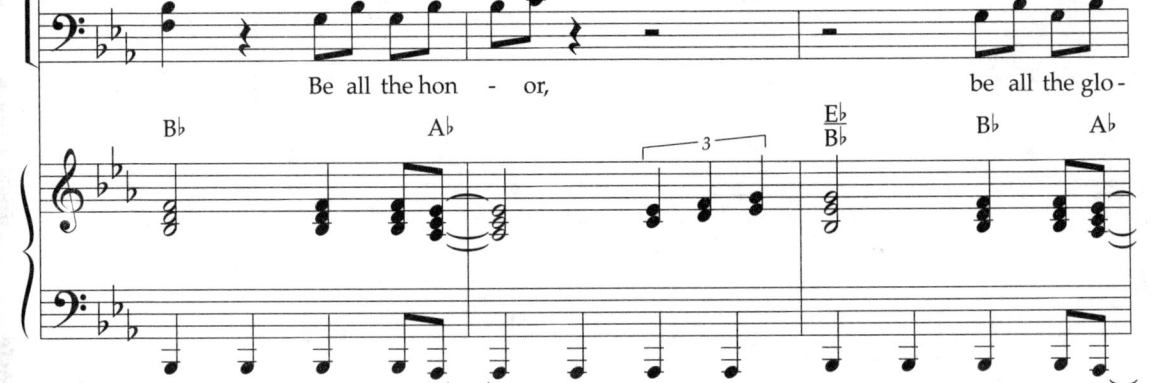

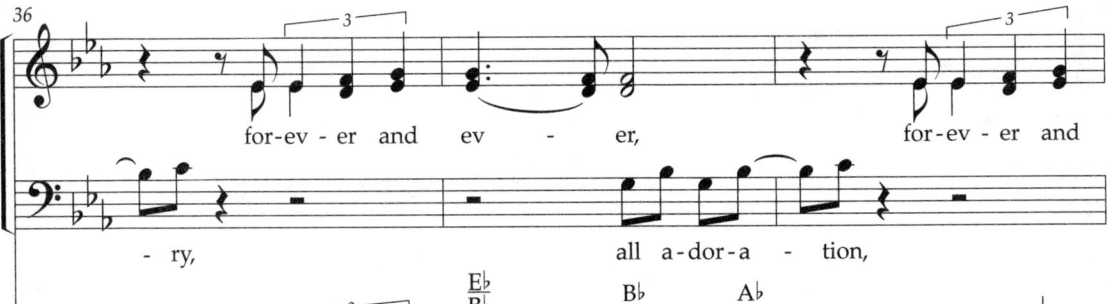

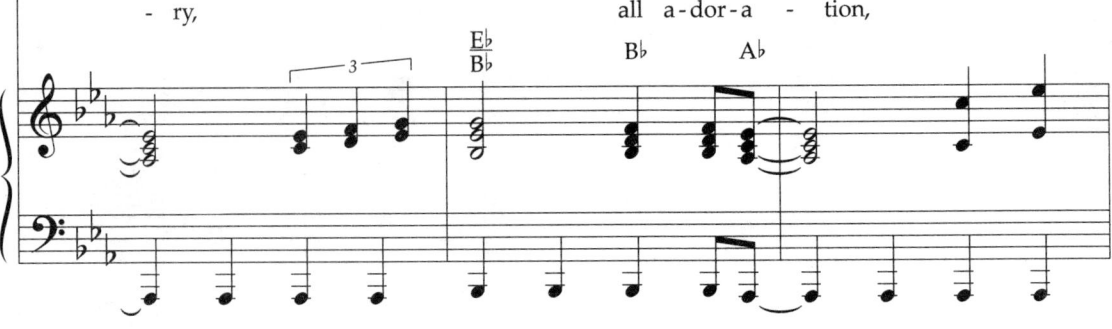

136

138

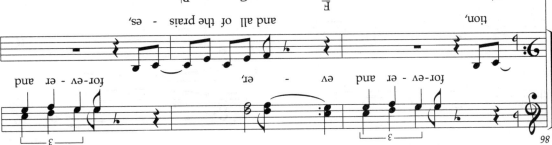

How Deep the Father's Love for Us

(SATB)

Words and Music by
STUART TOWNEND
Arranged by J. Daniel Smith

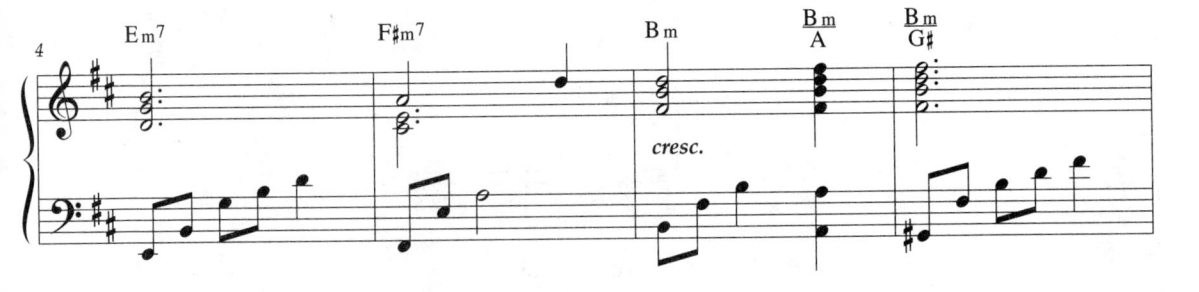

"Near the Cross," Music by William H. Doane.

© Copyright 1995 and this arr. © Copyright 2001 Kingsway's Thankyou Music (adm. in the Western Hemisphere by EMI Christian Music Publishing)/ASCAP. All rights reserved. Used by permission.

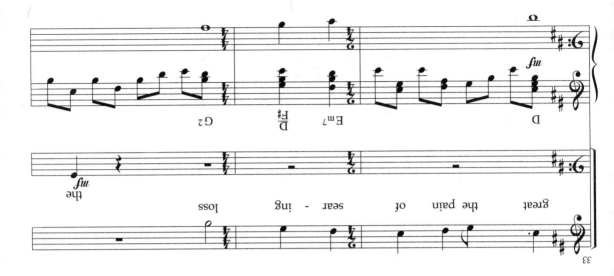

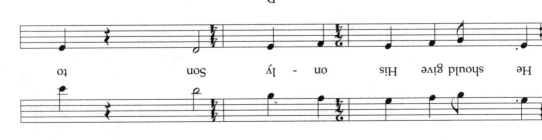

146

Fa - ther turns His face a - way. As

wounds which mar the Cho - sen One bring

man - y sons to glo - ry.

148

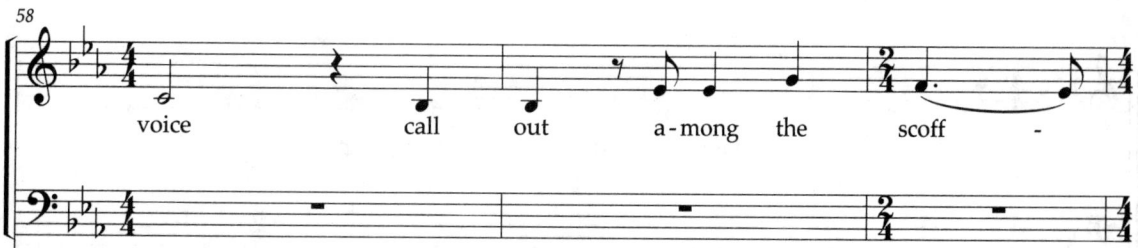

ders; A - shamed, I hear my mock - ing

voice call out a-mong the scoff -

ers. It was my sin that held Him

thing,   no gifts,   no pow'r, no   wis -

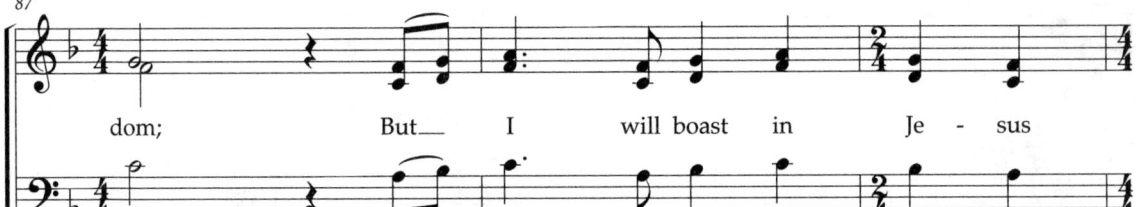

dom;   But___ I   will boast in   Je - sus

Christ,   His   death   and res - ur - rec -

152

tion. Why should I gain from His re-

ward? I can - not give an an -

swer. But this I know with all my

153

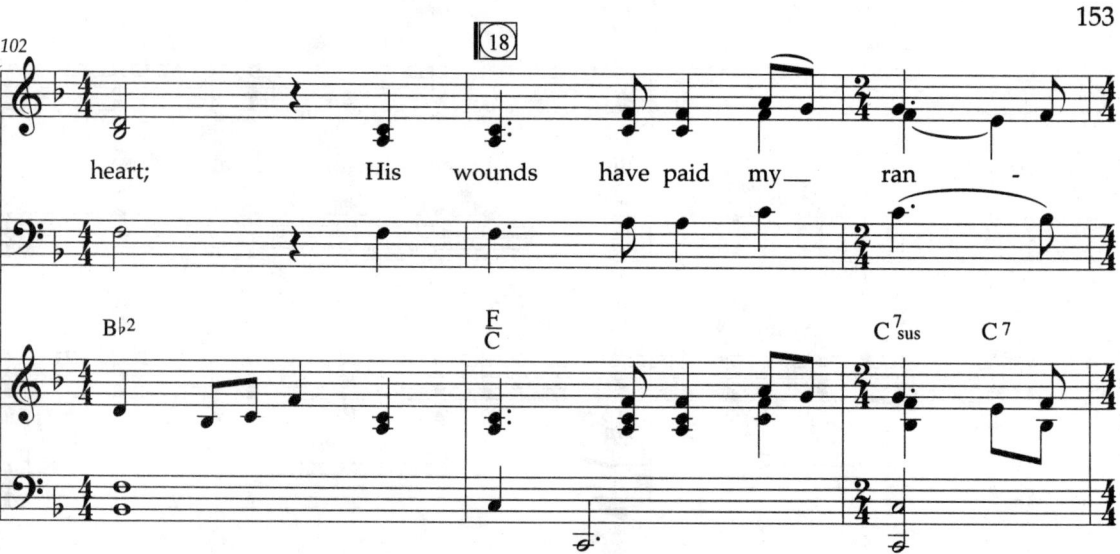

heart; His wounds have paid my ___ ran -

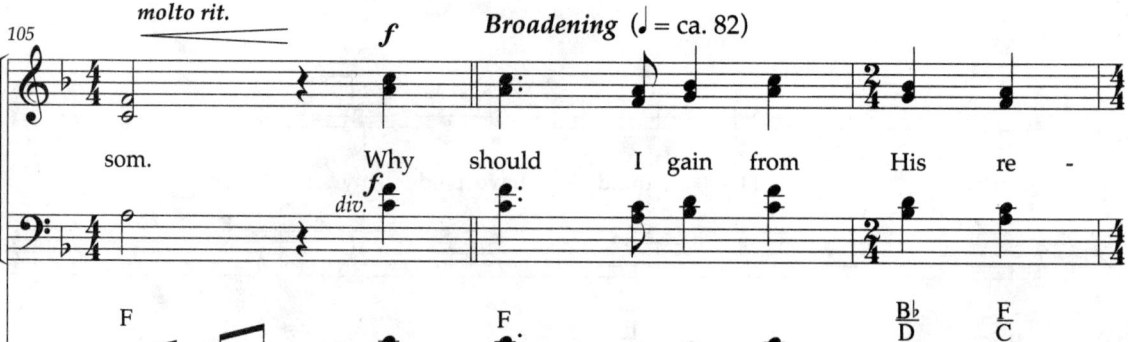

som. Why should I gain from His re -

ward? I can - not give an an -

154

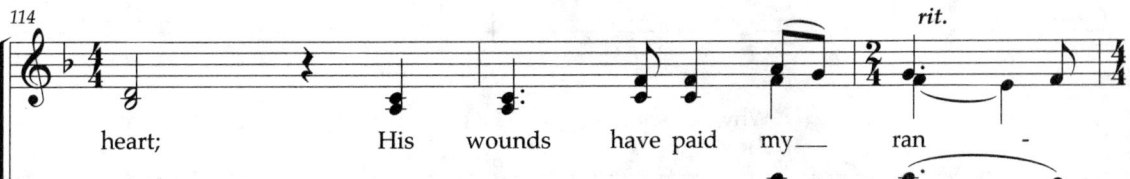

CHOIR *unis.*

heart; His wounds have paid my

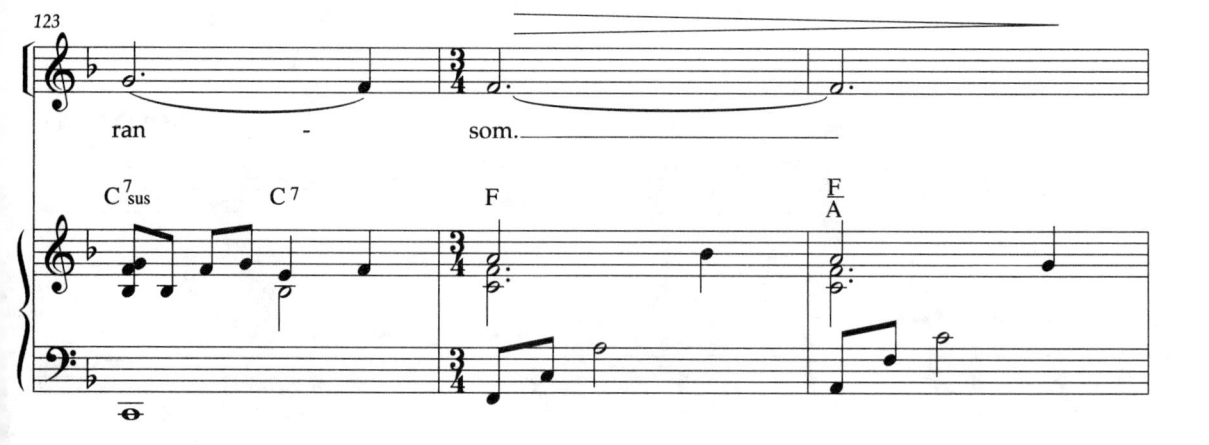

ran - som.

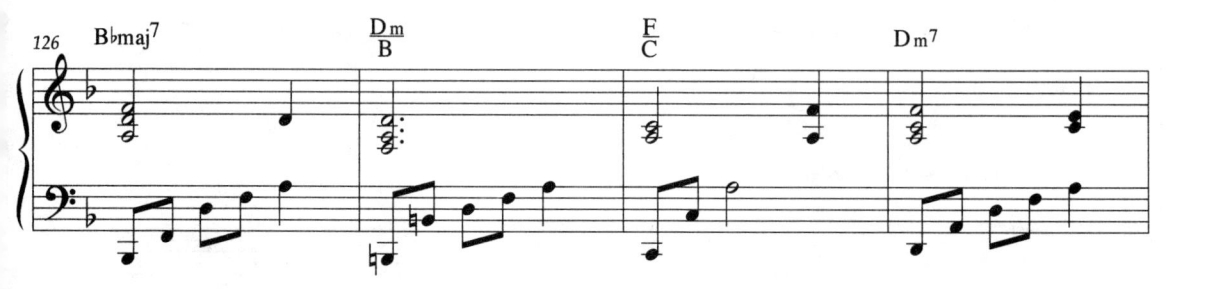

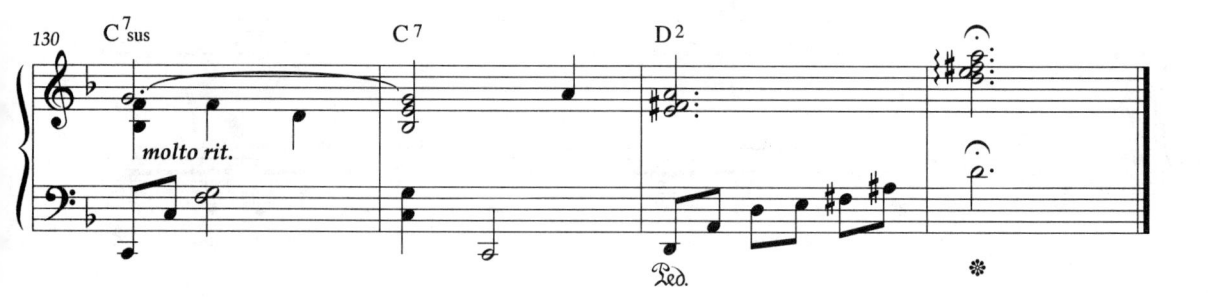

O Come, O Come, Emmanuel

(SSATB, Solos)

Plainsong
Arranged by Richard Kingsmore

Latin Hymn

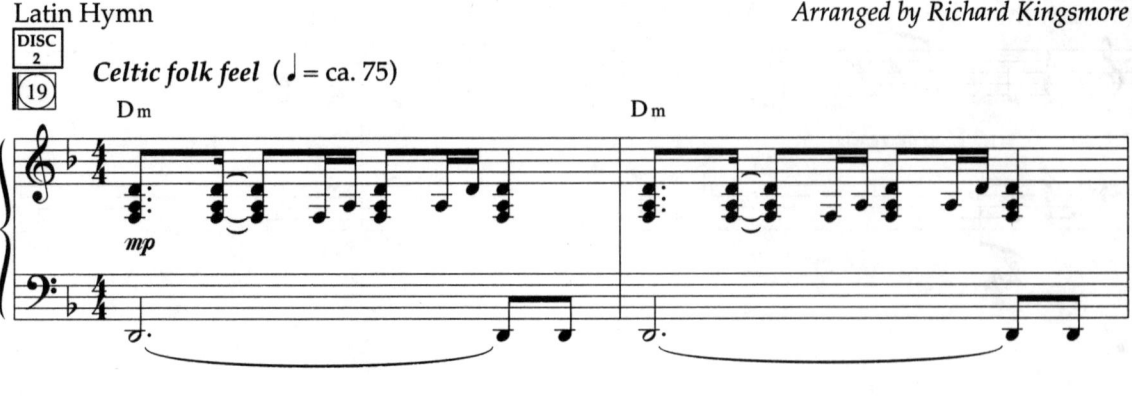

Arr. © Copyright 2002 Van Ness Press, Inc. (ASCAP).
All rights reserved.

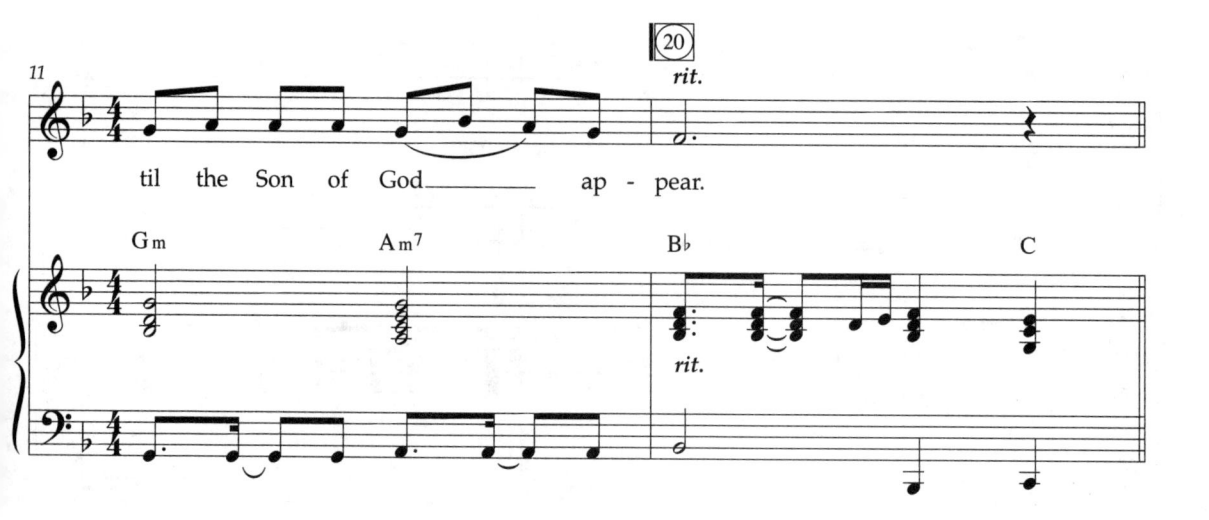

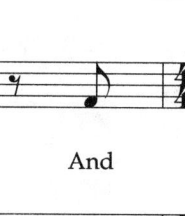

perse the gloom - y clouds_____ of night, And

death's dark shad - ows put_____ to flight. Re -

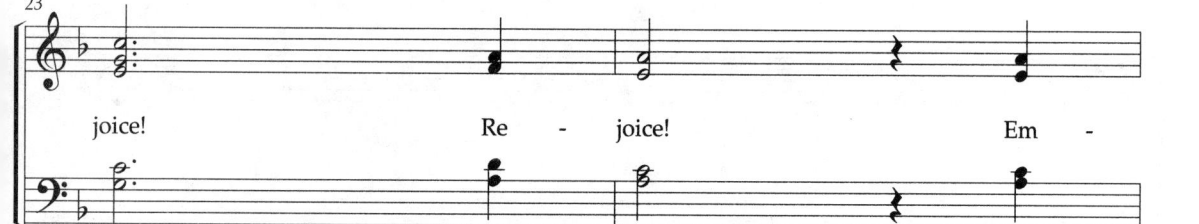

joice!   Re - joice!   Em -

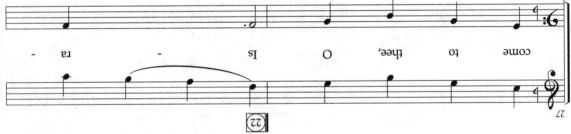
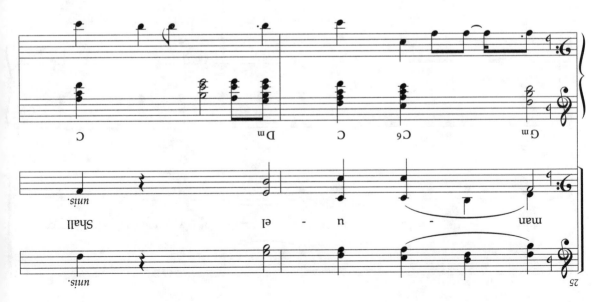

come to thee, O Is - ra - el!

O come, De - sire of na - tions,

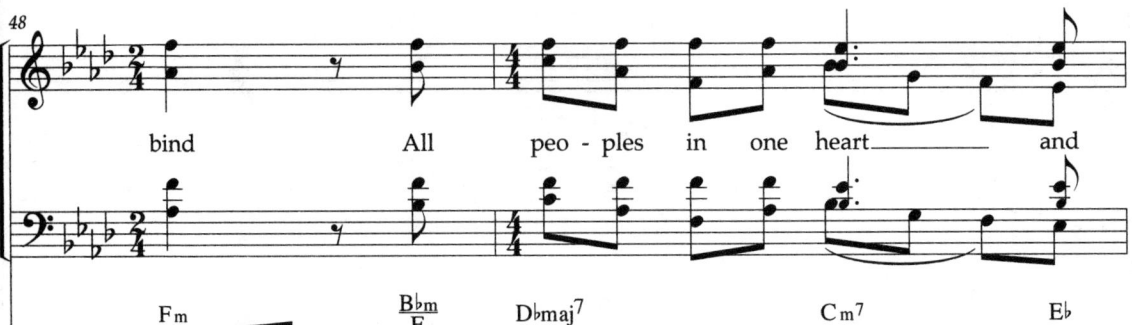

bind All peo - ples in one heart_____ and

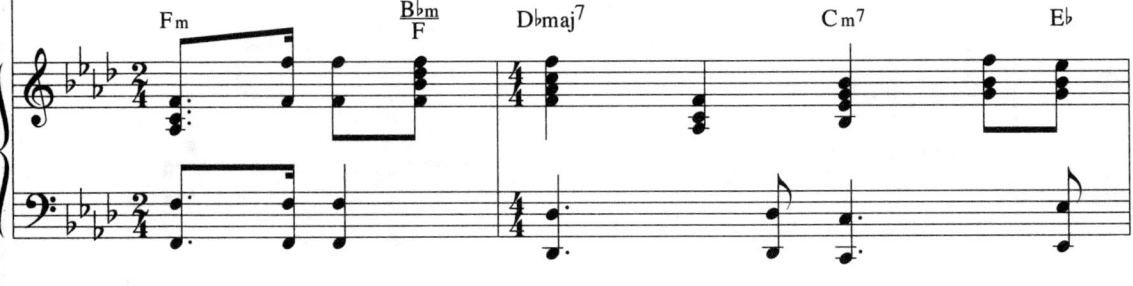

Silent Night, Holy Night
(SATB)

JOSEPH MOHR

FRANZ GRUBER
Arranged by Richard Kingsmore

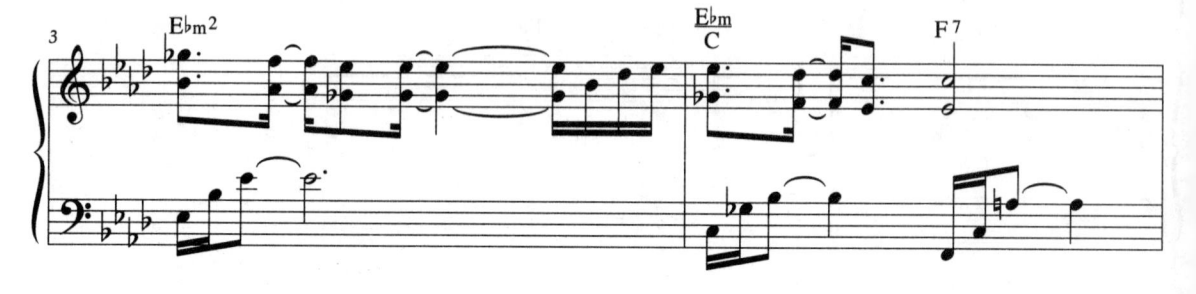

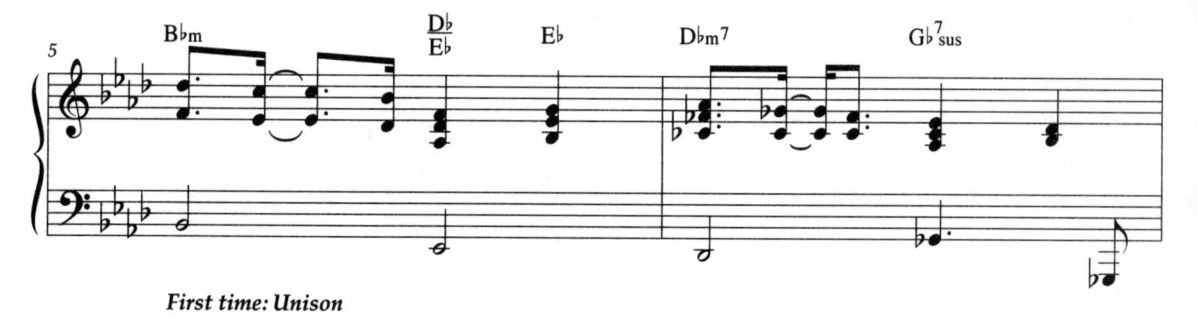

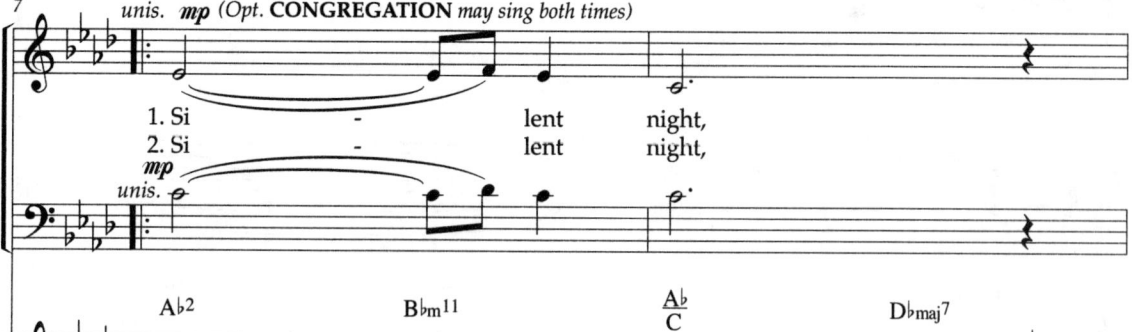

Arr. © Copyright 2002 Van Ness Press, Inc. (ASCAP).
All rights reserved.

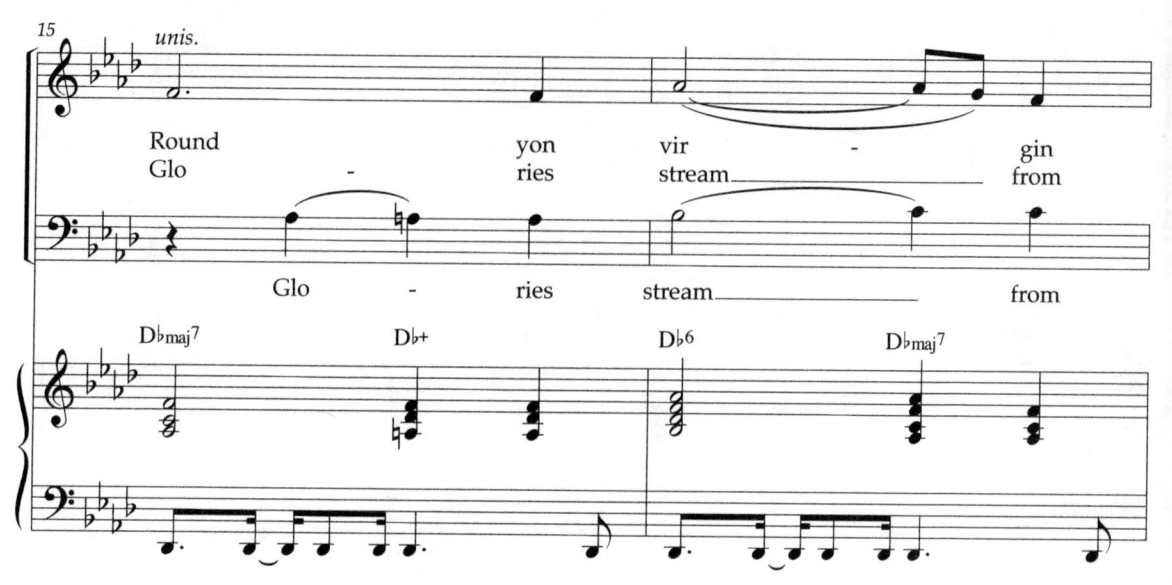

172

Sleep _____ in the heav - en - ly
Christ _____ the Sav - ior is

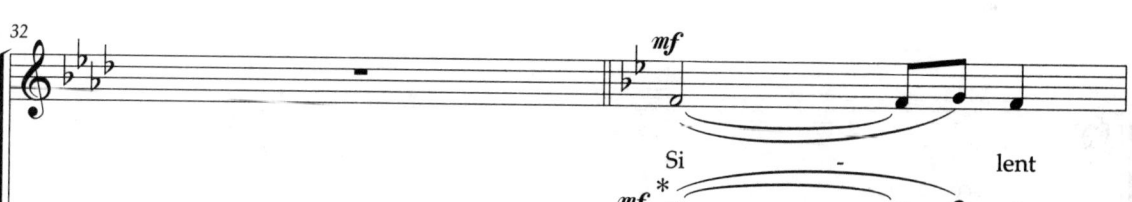

peace.

born!

Si - lent

*If tessitura is too high, basses sing melody.

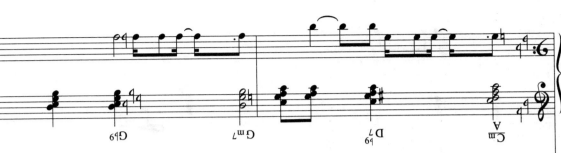
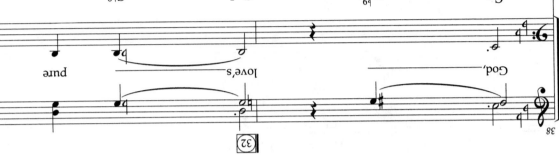

My Lips Will Praise You
(SATB)

Words and Music by
TWILA PARIS
Arranged by Bruce Greer

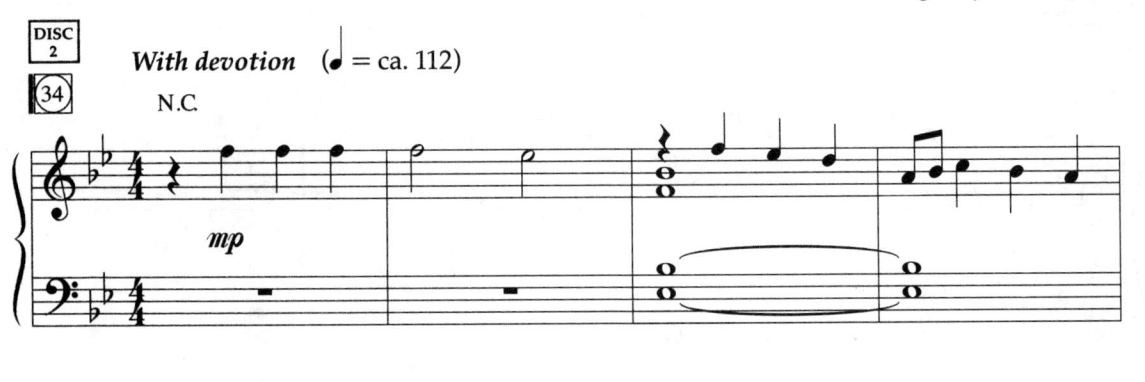

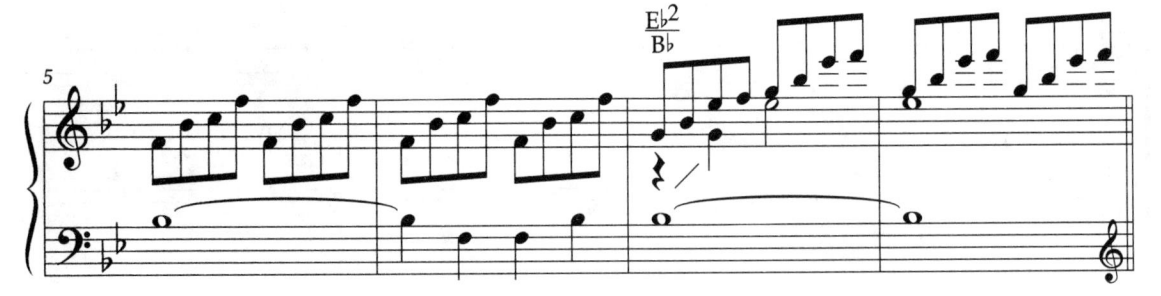

© Copyright 1998 Ariose Music/Mountain Spring Music (ASCAP). All rights administered by EMI Christian Music Publishing. All rights reserved. Used by permission.

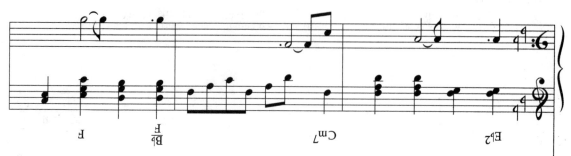
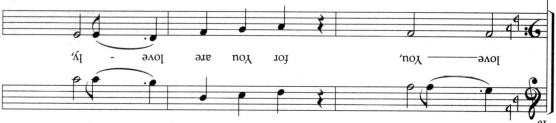

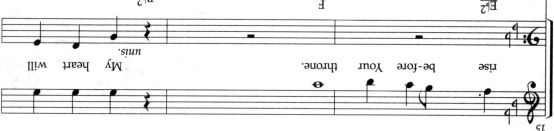

and You have called me to be - come Your____ own.

My lips will praise____ You,   for You are

ho - ly.　My voice will ev - er

rise be-fore Your throne.　　　My heart will

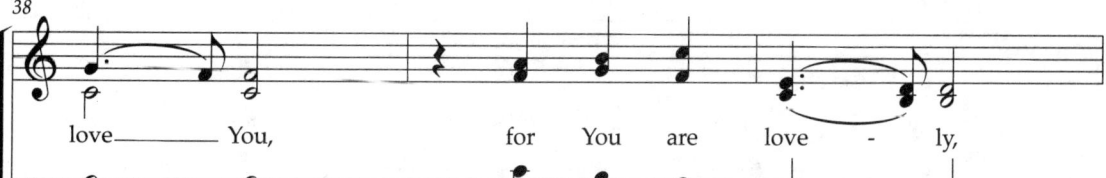

love　　You,　　for You are love - ly,

The King of Love
(SATB)

Words and Music by
STUART TOWNEND
and KEVIN JAMIESON
Arranged by J. Daniel Smith

Joyfully (♩ = ca. 130)

© Copyright 1997 and this arr. © Copyright 2001 Kingsway's Thankyou Music
(admin. in the Western Hemisphere by EMI Christian Music Publishing)/ASCAP.
All rights reserved. Used by permission.

CHOIR *unis.*

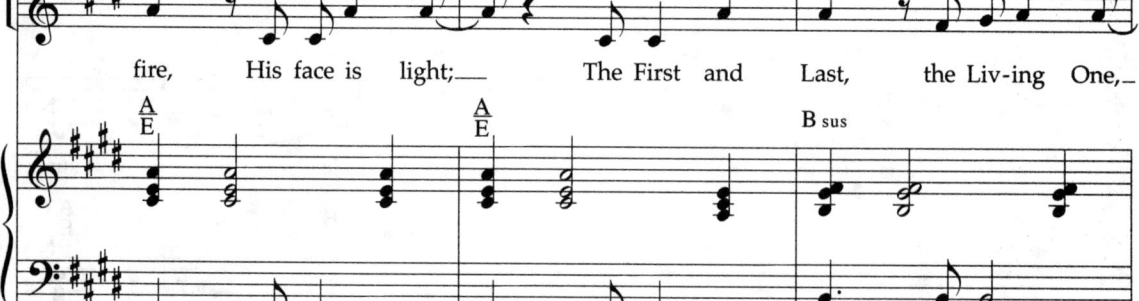

The King of love is my de - light,___ His eyes are

fire, His face is light;___ The First and Last, the Liv-ing One,___

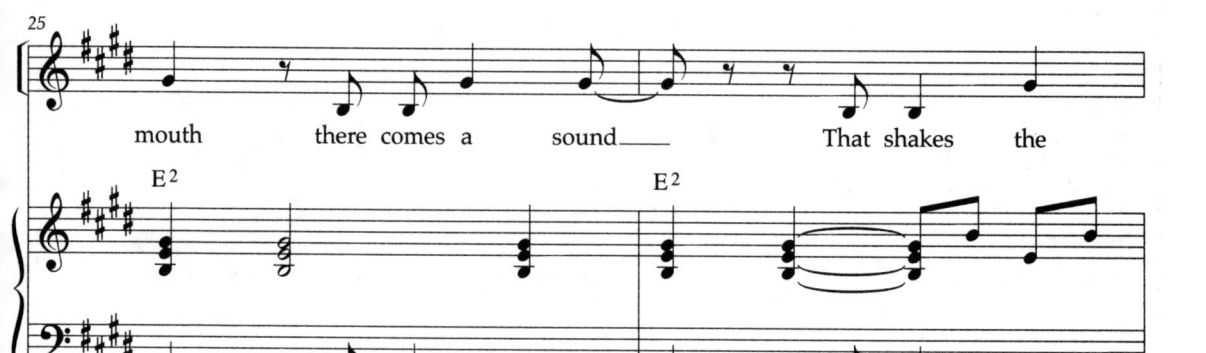

— His name is Je - sus.___ And from His

mouth there comes a sound___ That shakes the

190

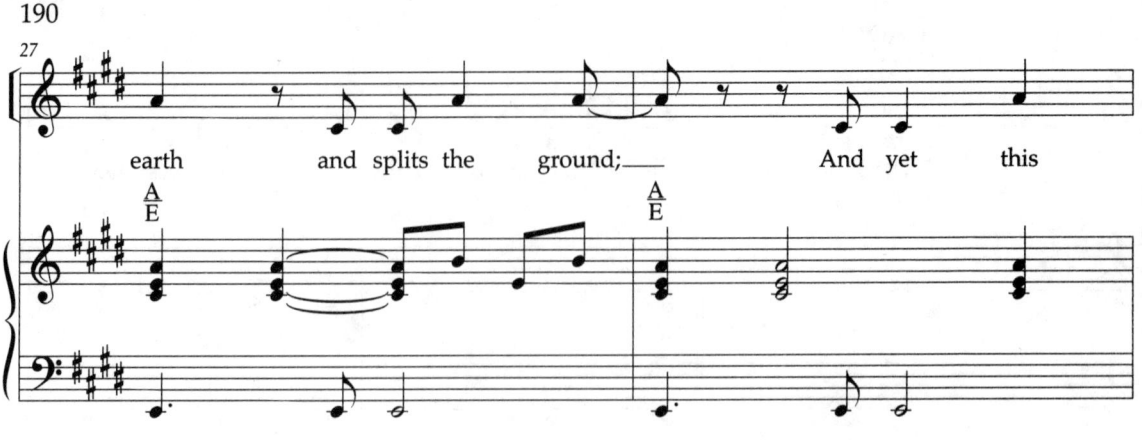

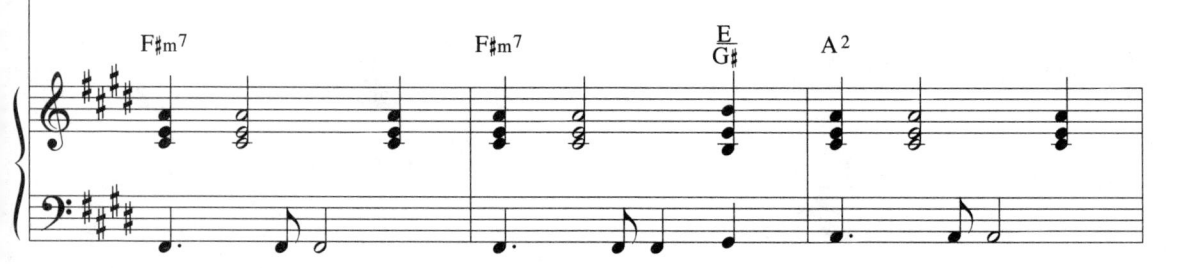

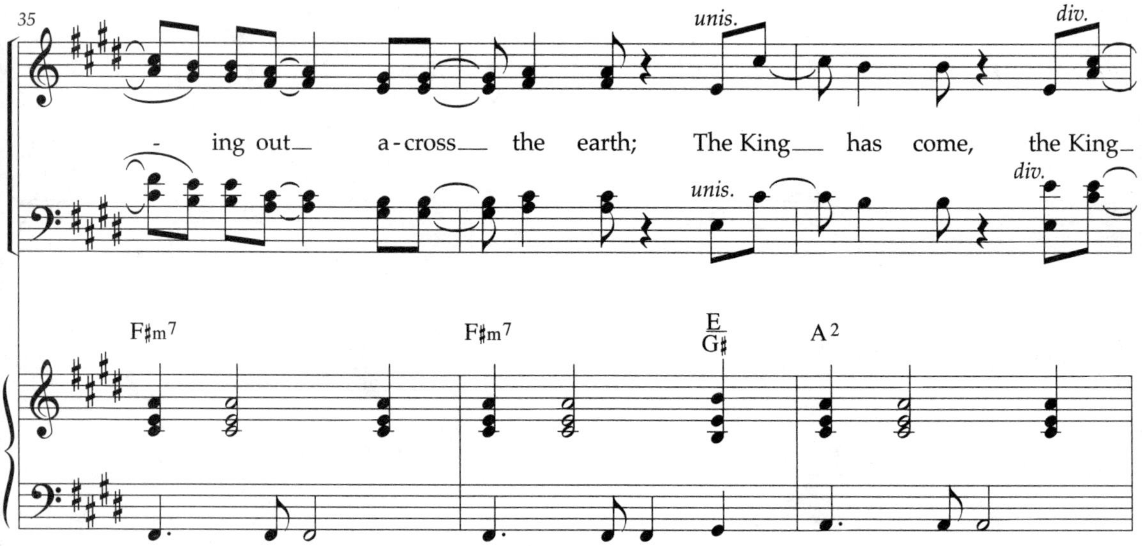
35
unis.
div.
- ing out a-cross the earth; The King has come, the King
unis.
div.
F♯m7
F♯m7
E/G♯
A2

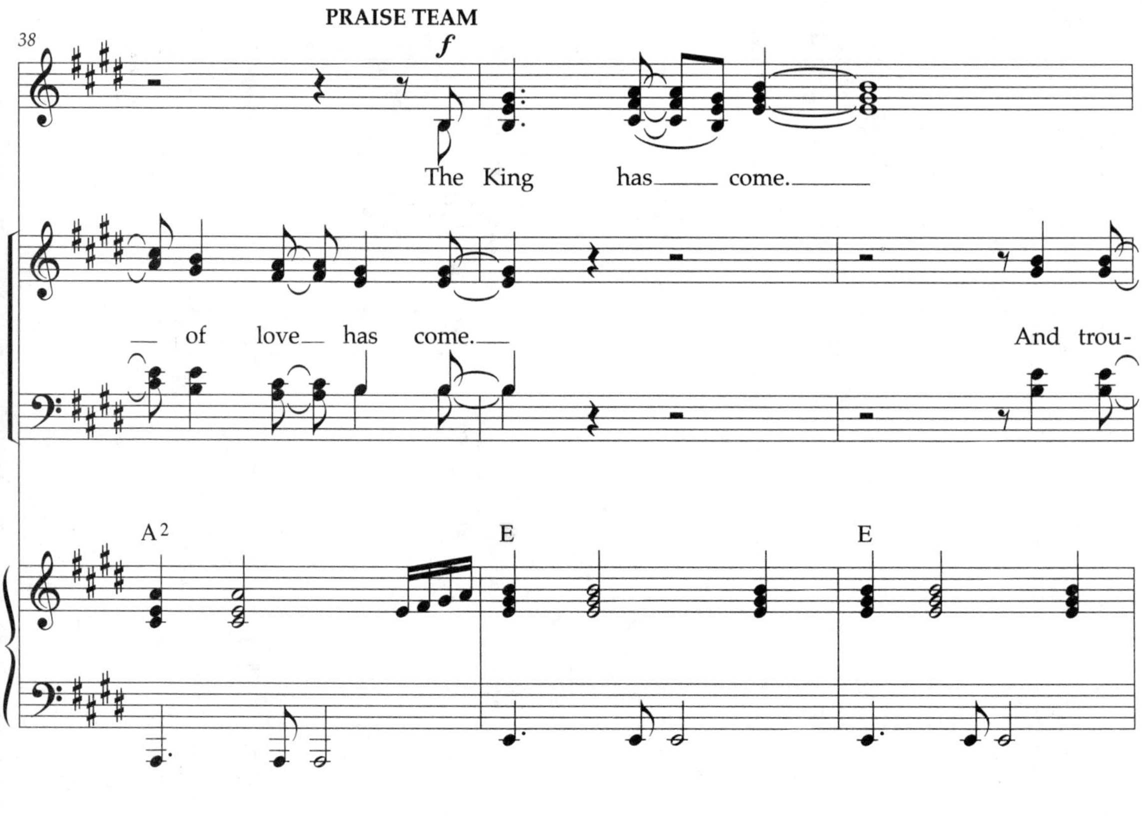
38
PRAISE TEAM
f
The King has come.
of love has come. And trou-
A2
E
E

192

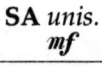

SA *unis.*
mf

47

My lov - er's breath is sweet-est wine,—

decresc.

E   E   E^2

mf

50

— I am His prize and He is mine;—

E^2 $\frac{A}{E}$

52

— How can a sin - ner know such joy?— Be-cause of

$\frac{A}{E}$ B sus   B sus

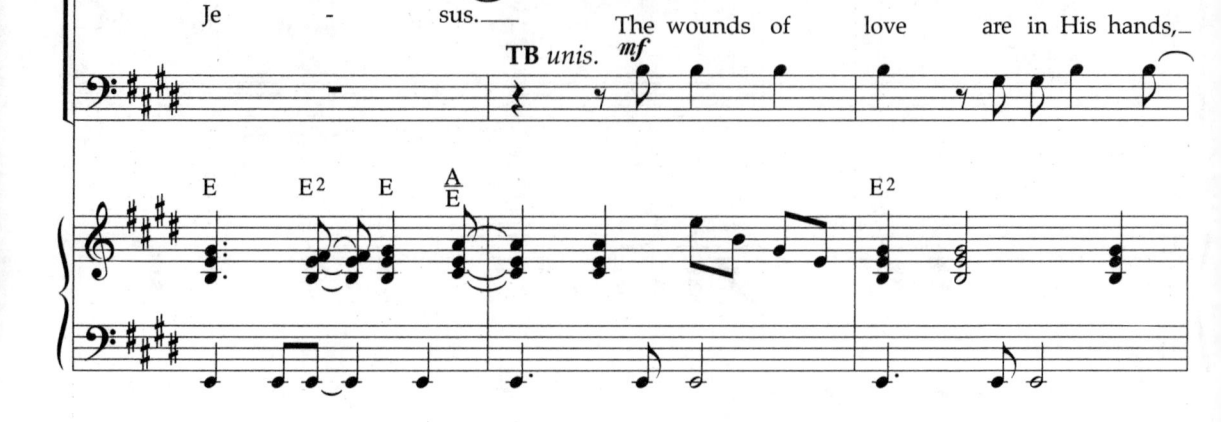

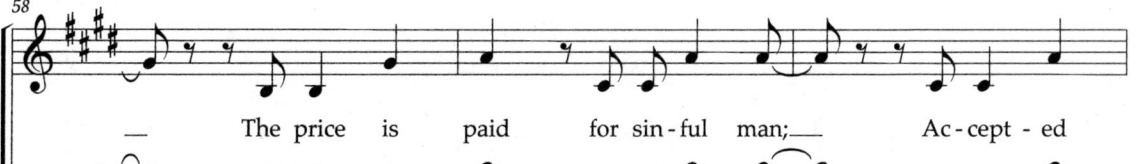

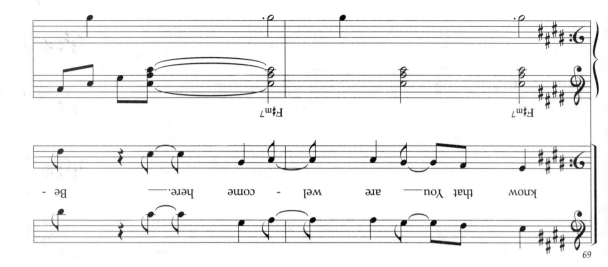
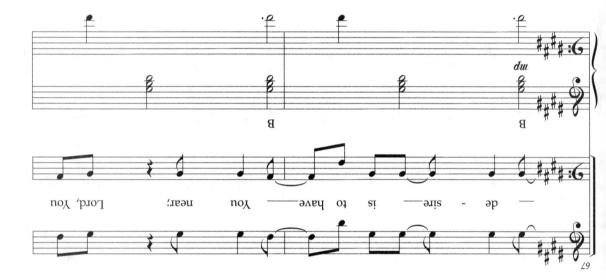

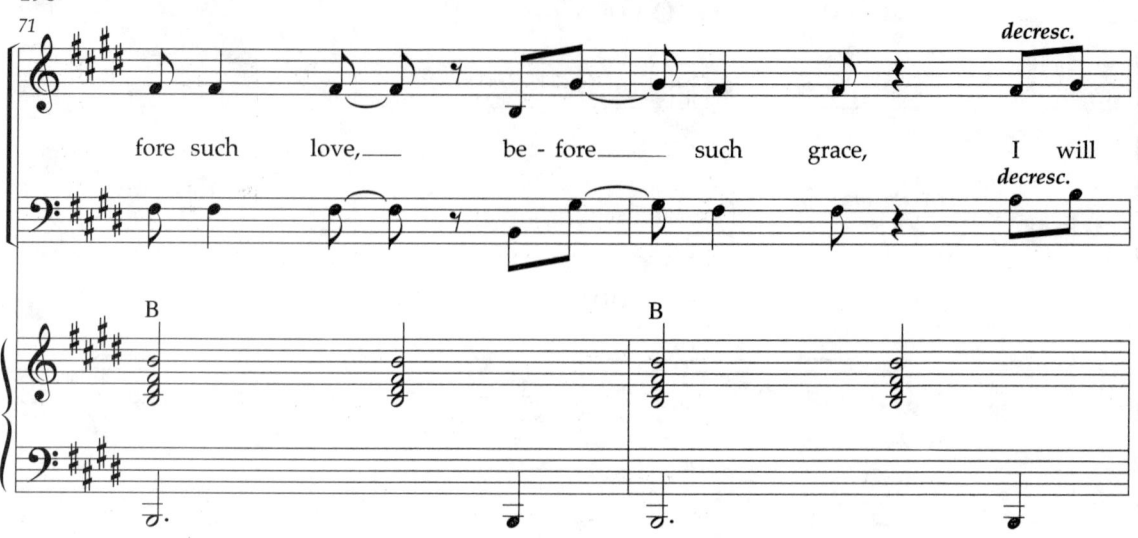

fore such love,_____ be - fore_____ such grace, I will

let the walls_ come down._____ I will

let the walls_ come down._____

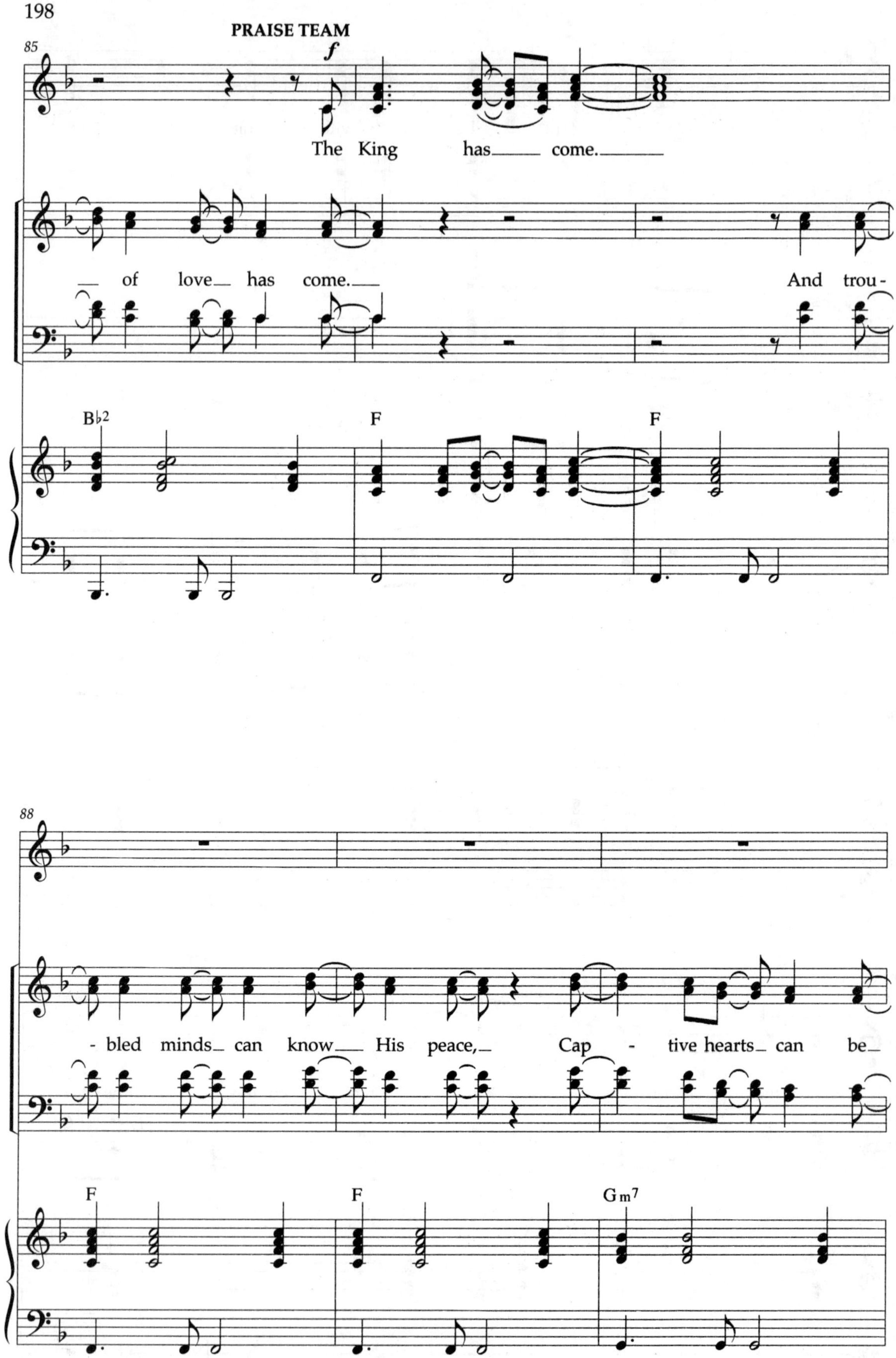

PRAISE TEAM

The King has____ come.____

____ of love__ has come.____   And trou-

- bled minds__ can know____ His peace,____ Cap - tive hearts__ can be__

96

Sing— my songs.—

—will sing— my songs— of love,— Call - ing out— a - cross—

F   F   G m7

99

unis.   div.

— the earth; The King— has come,   the King— of love— has come.—

unis.   div.

G m7   F/A   B♭2   B♭2

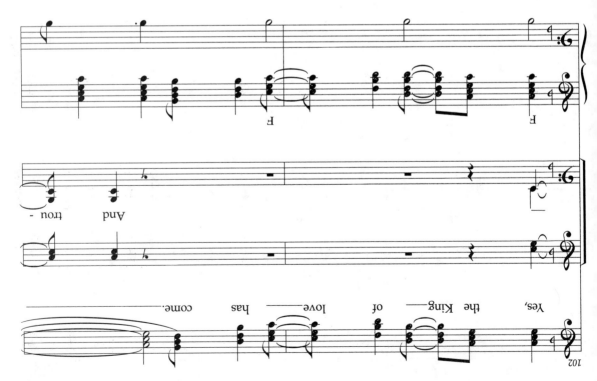

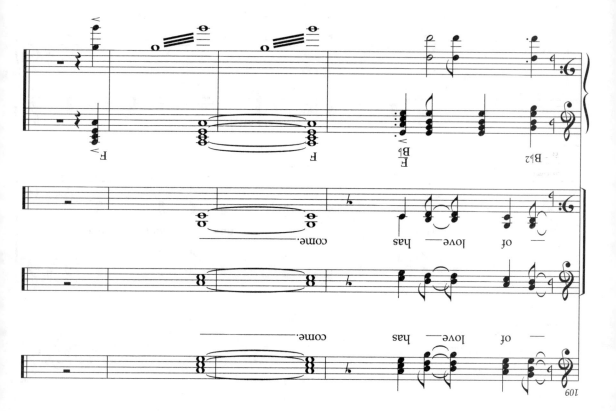

Be
(SATB)

Words and Music by
ROBERT WHITE JOHNSON
and JIM ROBINSON
Arranged by J. Daniel Smith

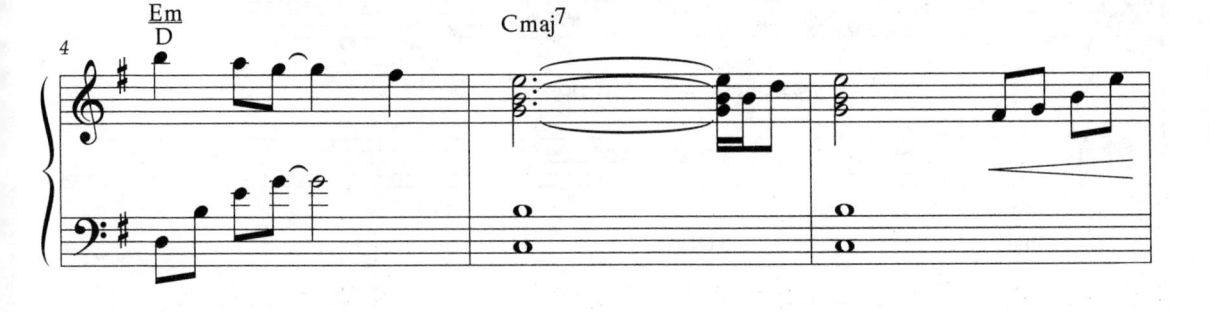

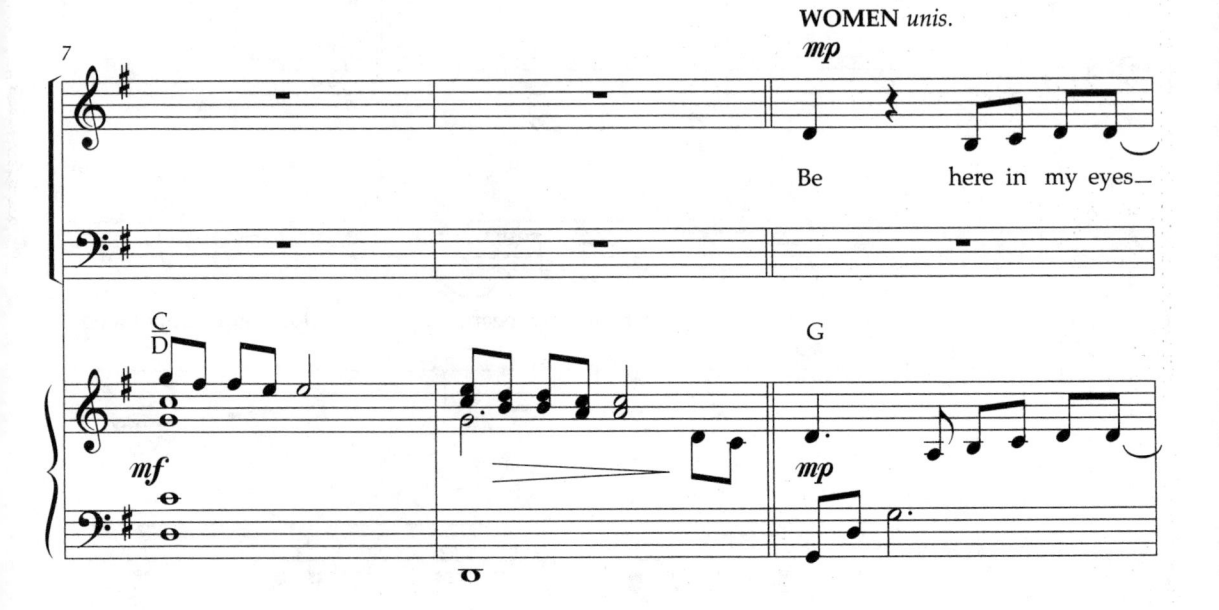

© Copyright 1999 RadioQuest Music Publishing (BMI)/ProdigalSong Music.
All rights reserved. Used by permission.

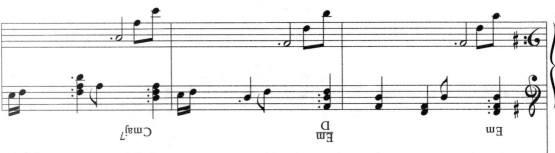

-fort and__ to build__ shel-ter for those__ who need__ Your love..

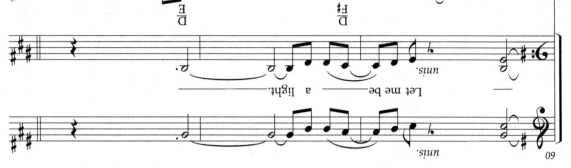

You Are Worthy
(SATB)

Words and Music by
DAN R. EDWARDS
Arranged by Russell Mauldin

© Copyright 1998 Broadman Press (SESAC).
All rights reserved.

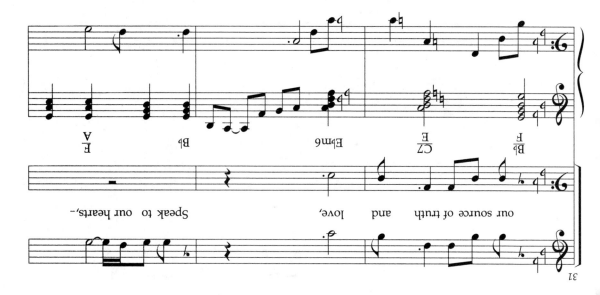

216

218

55
unis.
wor - thy to— be praised,— wor - thy of— de - vo - tion and the
unis.
F/A C/G F C/E
57
div.
songs our voic - es raise. You are wor - thy—
div.
Dm11 C/D F/G G F/G G C G/B
59
unis.
now and ev - er - more; You are wor - thy,— You're wor - thy to— be
unis.
F/A C/G C C/E Dm7 Fadd9/G G

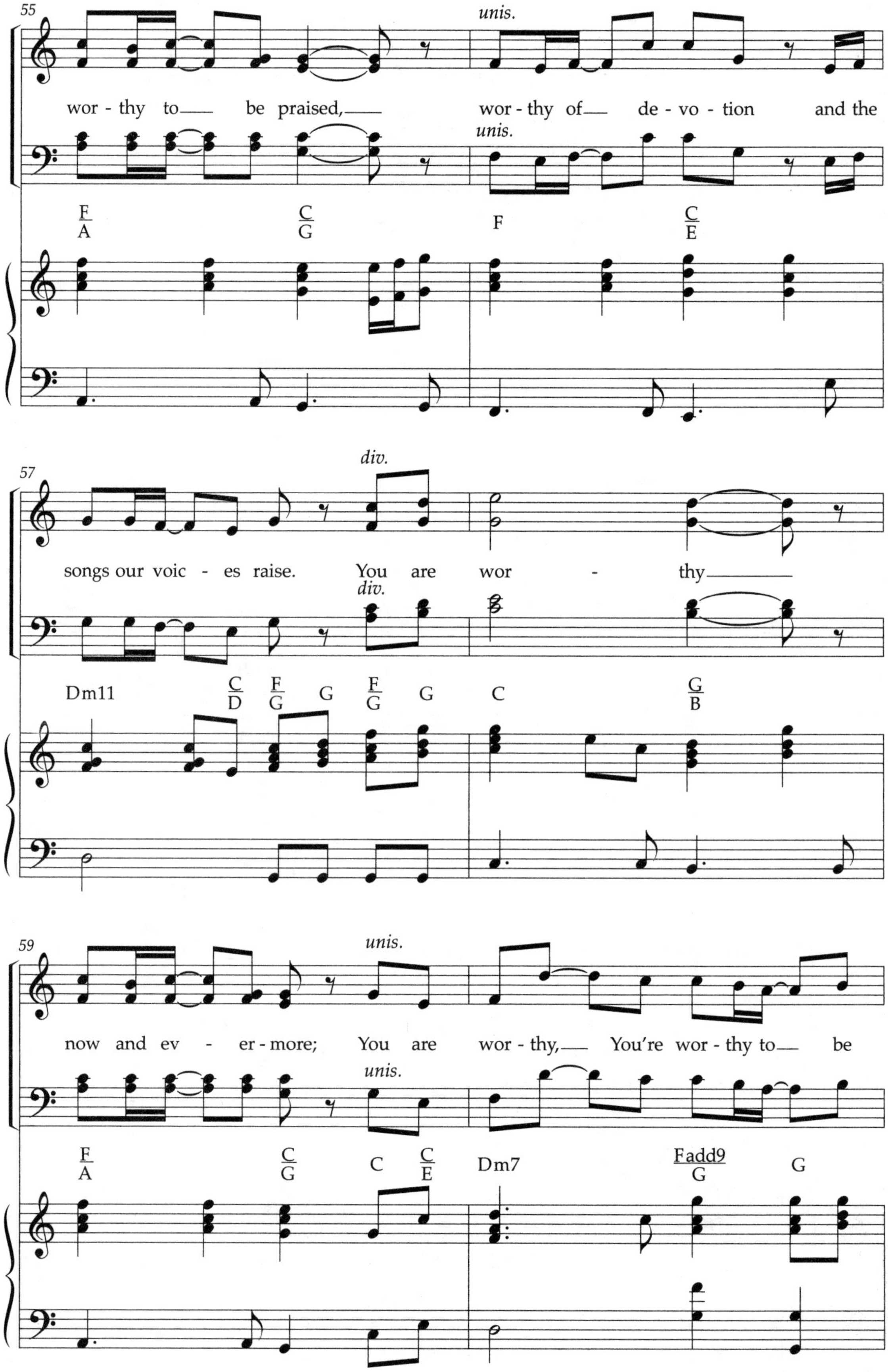

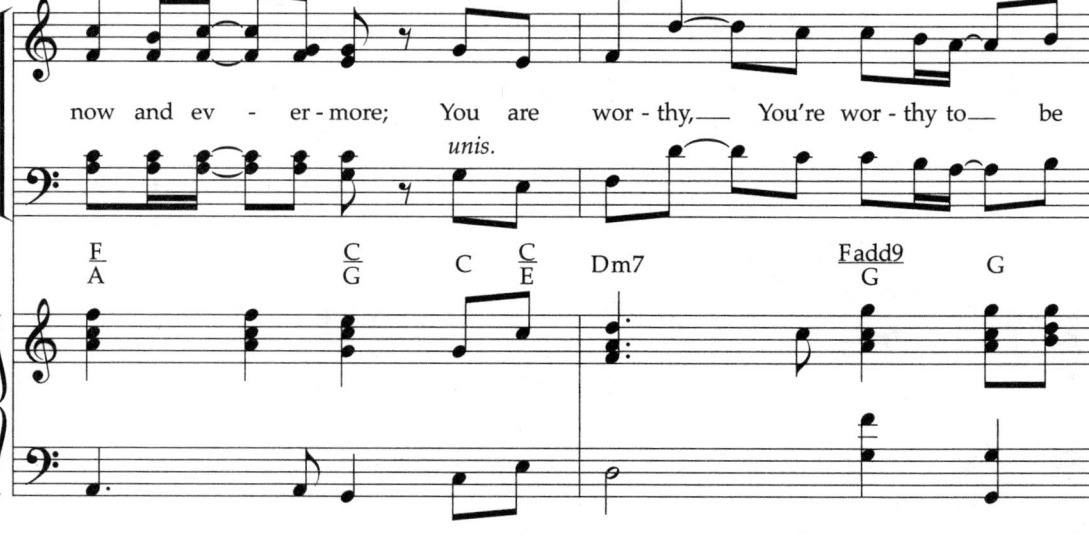

We Are the Body of Christ

(SATB)

Words and Music by
SCOTT WESLEY BROWN
and DAVID HAMPTON
Arranged by Bruce Greer

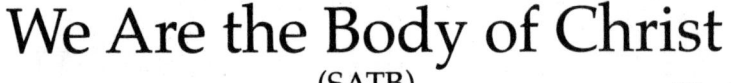

DISC 2 54

With resolve (♩ = ca. 60)

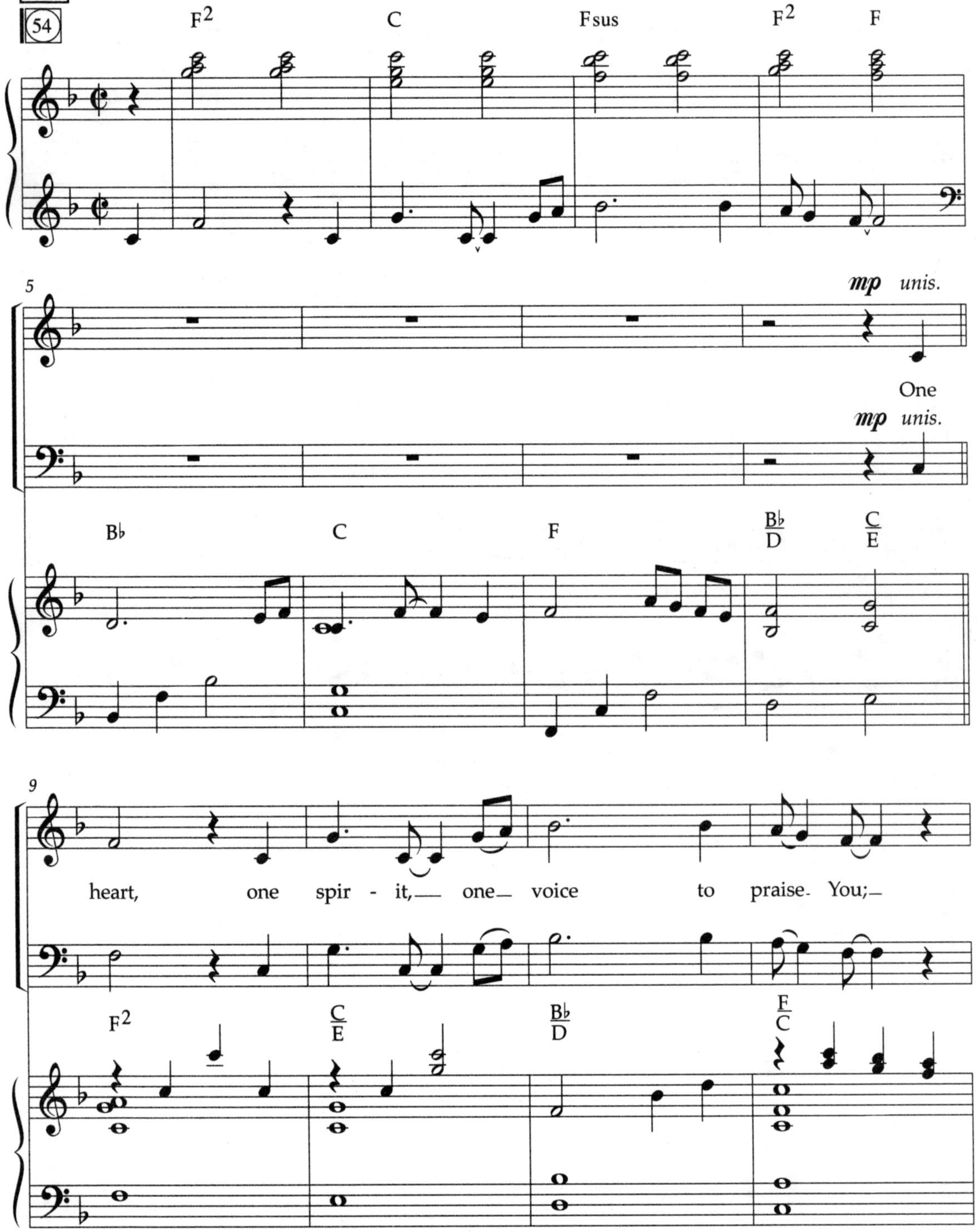
F2
C
Fsus
F2
F
5
mp unis.
One
mp unis.
B♭
C
F
B♭/D
C/E
9
heart, one spir - it, one voice to praise. You;
F2
C/E
B♭/D
F/C

© Copyright 1997 Integrity's Hosanna! Music/ASCAP and New Spring Publishing (ASCAP) (admin. by Brentwood-Benson Music Publishing, Inc.)/Songward Music (ASCAP) (admin. by Music Services) and ThreeFold Amen Music, (c/o ROM Administration, 8315 Twin Lakes Drive, Mobile, AL 36695).
All rights reserved. Used by permission.

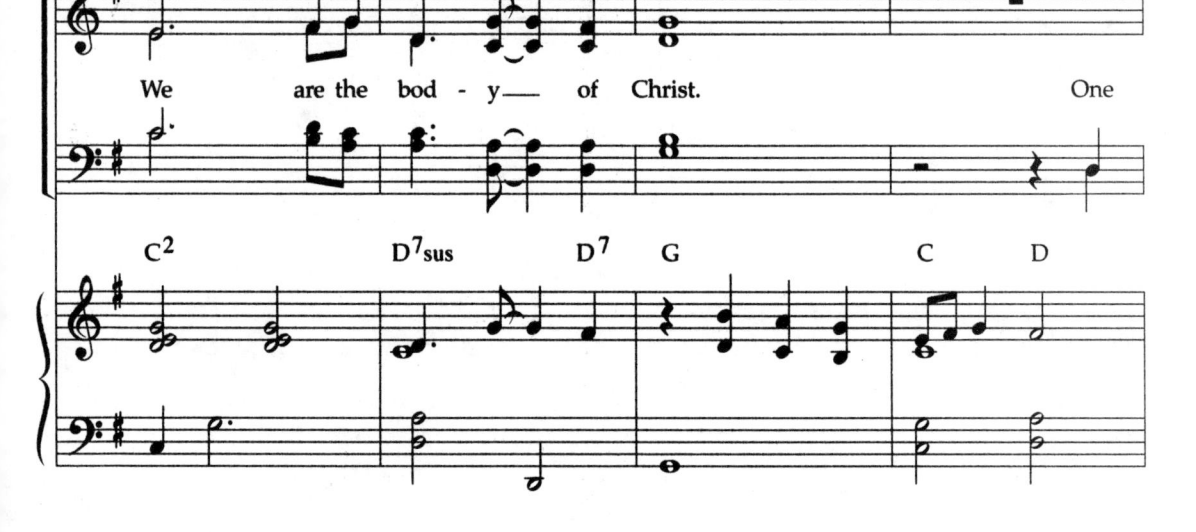

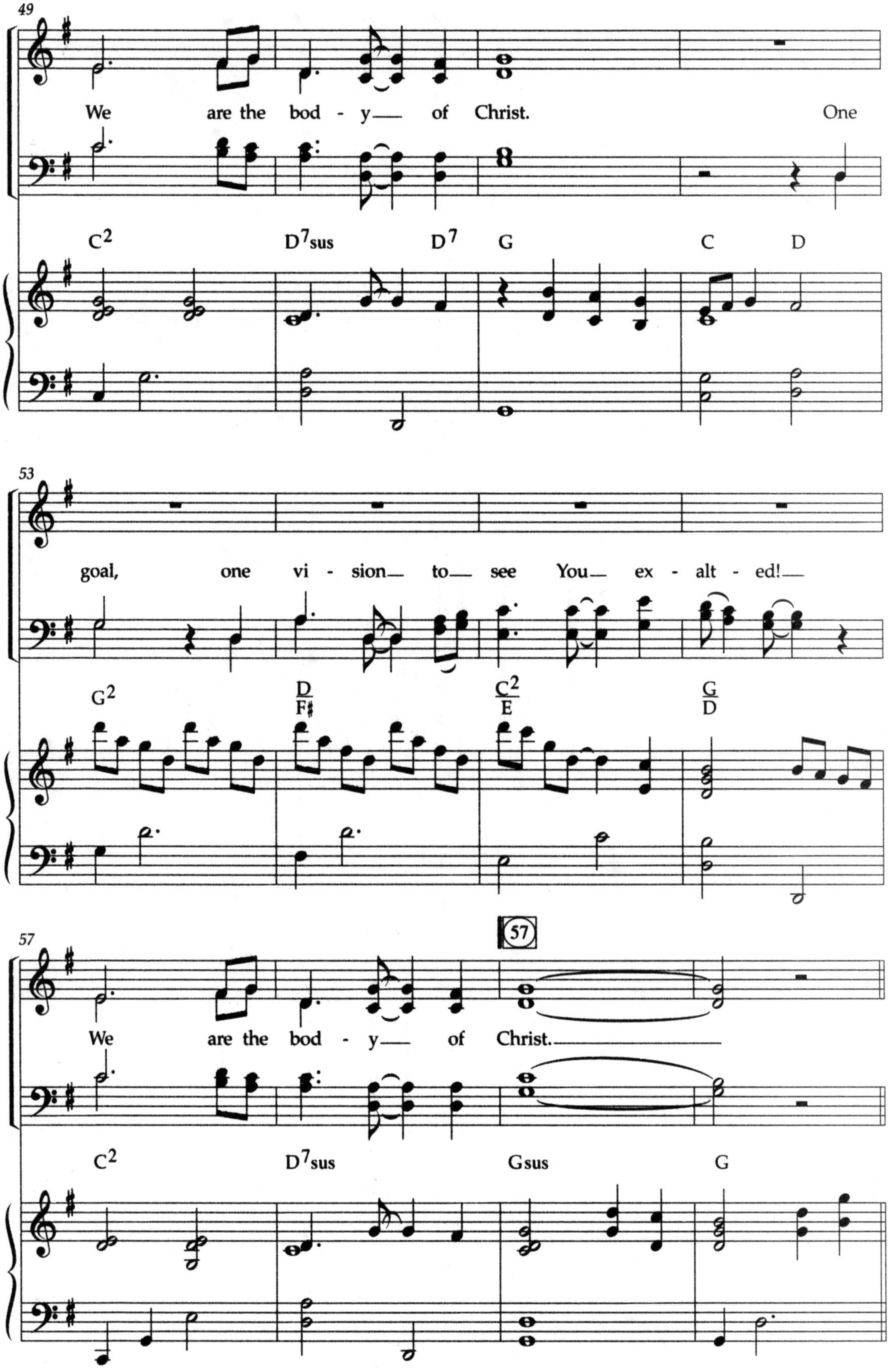
49
We are the bod - y of Christ. One
C2 D7sus D7 G C D
53
goal, one vi - sion to see You ex - alt - ed!
G2 D/F# C2/E G/D
57
57
We are the bod - y of Christ.
C2 D7sus Gsus G

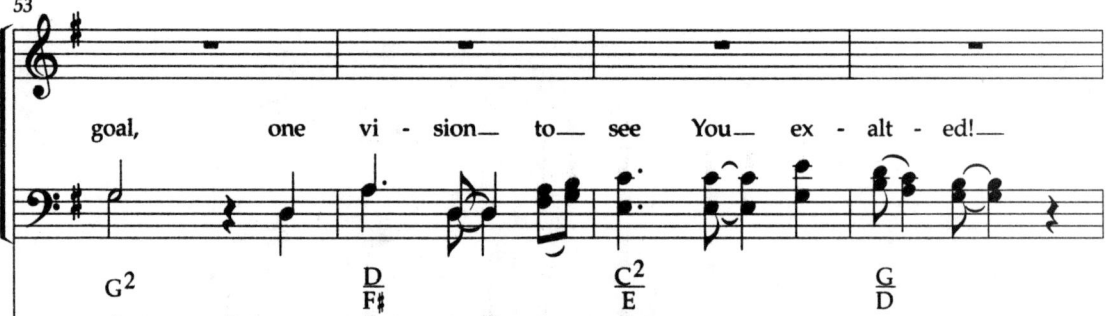

228

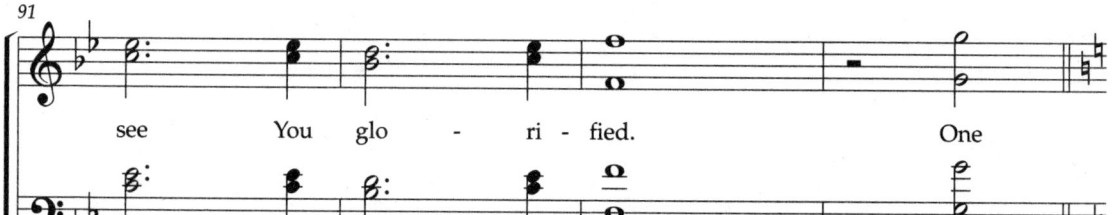

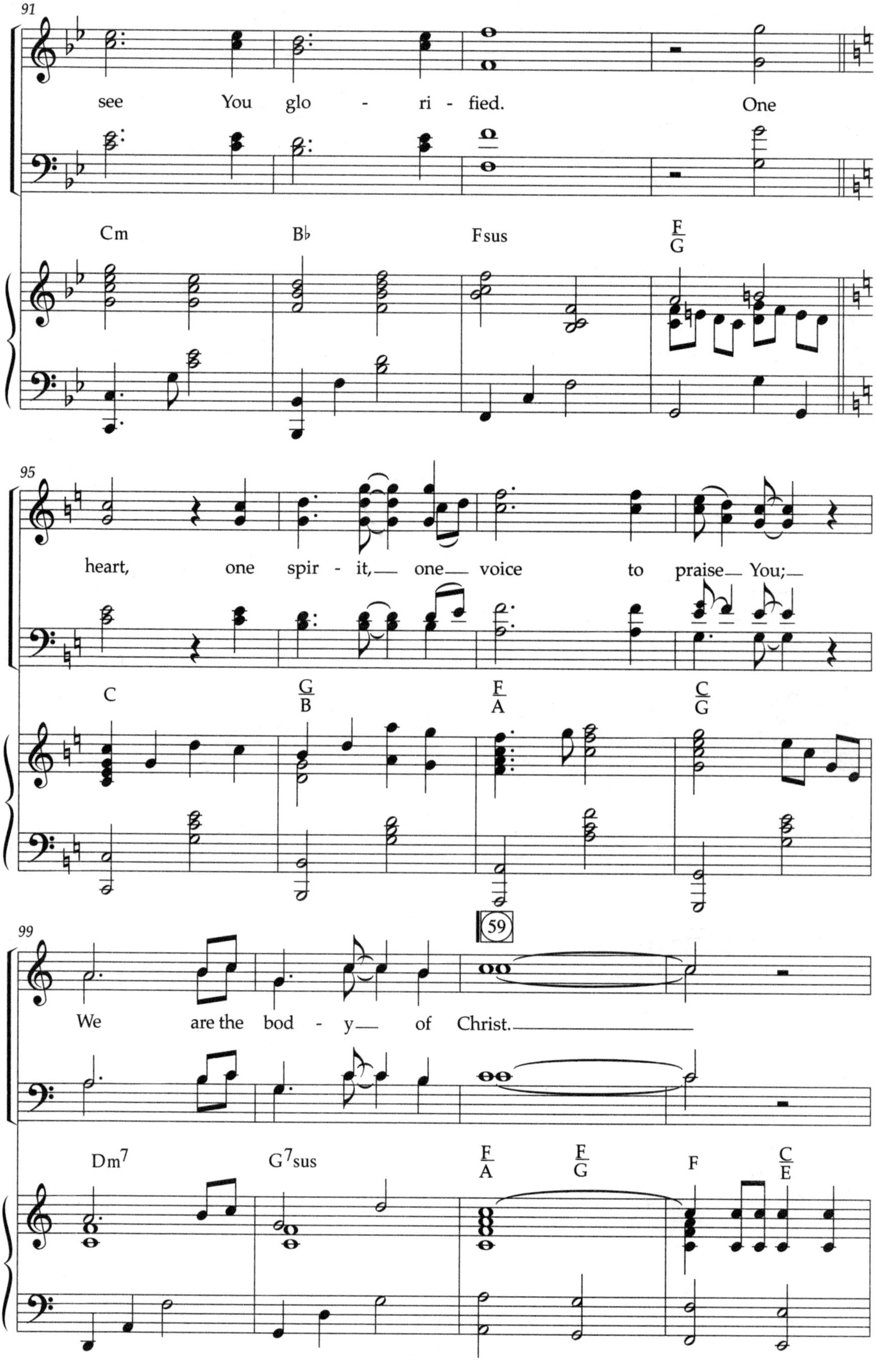
91
see You glo - ri - fied. One
Cm
B♭
Fsus
F/G
95
heart, one spir - it, one voice to praise You;
C
G/B
F/A
C/G
59
99
We are the bod - y of Christ.
Dm7
G7sus
F/A
F/G
F
C/E

Bow your head. Lift your voice. Worship!

Let the sounds of worship fill the air as you continue to rejoice in what God has done! Within these collections of praise and worship music for choir and congregation, you'll find popular selections, created and arranged by some of today's most talented writers and musicians. Contemporary, rhythm-driven songs with dynamic accompaniment give you the means to let the praises ring out!